FINDING VERN

Darcy Bellows-Mascorro

ISBN-13:978-0615932132 (Blue Dove Media)
ISBN-10:0615932134

CREDITS

Contributing Editors:

Amanda Brown

Adrian Reynolds

Charlene Melson

Evidential Spiritual Mediums:

Michelle Tedrow

Vickie Gay

Bernie Scott

Jacqueline Murray

DEDICATION

To my beloved in heaven, you rocked my world, you are my everything. This one's for you my hero. Until we meet again you are forever in my heart.

PROLOGUE

For one beaming starlit moment in time, I was truly blessed. I had happy children, and we had survived a few challenges. I had the love and support of the man of my dreams. We were living in a beautiful home in a pretty town. This peace, this dream, had not come easily, nor was it easy to maintain. However, it was something I enjoyed with every fiber of my being.

I truly looked forward to getting home every night. As soon as the clock hit six, it was like being released from prison and going home to the magic kingdom. I could never get enough. Each morning when I left for work, I felt like a kid who didn't want to leave the park because I was having too much fun. I still got butterflies and welled with excitement at the first sight of the man I loved so dearly.

Imagine coming home one night and the enchanted castle you had spent your life creating was burned to the ground with no chance of reconstruction.

I bring you my story of love and loss in order to share with you the hope I was given to carry on through the darkest of tragedies.

CHAPTER 1: THE JOURNEY TO US

I grew up living in the love of the common people. My mom and dad lived a few blocks apart from one another in a blue-collar town nestled between the banks of two rivers in Minnesota. The town was called Anoka, a Native American word for working waters or two sides of the river. It was a pretty lumber town that was almost 200 years old.

My mom, Jan, was a smart, shy, pretty girl. She didn't know what she wanted to be when she grew up. She was an artist but never felt she was good enough to make money at it. She liked hanging out with close friends and family. My dad, Don, was a rebel. He moved out of his family home at 15 because he didn't like following house rules...at least that's what grandpa said. He looked a little like Elvis and sounded just like Johnny Cash and Waylon Jennings when he sang.

When Dad was 17 and Mom was 19, Dad gave Mom a ride home from a party one night...and that was it. They got together then, and they're still together now. Mom got pregnant with me in short order. I became the first child of very young parents, the first to enter Mom and Dad's social group. I was the party baby, little Darcy who all the young people played with on the weekends and the occasional weeknight after a day of hard labor.

Being the center of attention for not only my mom and dad, but the group of friends they spent their free time with, my young family life was filled with celebration. Dad played the guitar and sang for friends and family almost every weekend when they were young, and I always felt like he was singing just for me.

"Daddy's going to buy you a dream to cling to, momma's going to love you just as much as she can... and she can." I enjoyed music so much that at three years old, I had a picture of Johnny Cash by my bed. My baby brother was eleven months younger than me and became the sidekick in the adventures that I would invent for us. I took the hero role.

This hi-fi experience of the world would set the bar for the young me. I believed life was open to anything I set my eye on. I recall a line from my favorite poem, A Season in Hell by Arthur Rimbaud, "Once if I remember well, My life was a feast where all hearts were opened and all wines poured..." That's how life seemed to me, the young Darcy.

I truly felt anything was possible. My family made me feel like I was special enough to do anything. I grew up surrounded by a big support system. My aunt was my hero. Not only was she beautiful, but she was smart, an attorney who had traveled the world. Everyone liked to hear her perspective on things because she was so educated and articulate. I wanted to be just like her. She warned me that there would be people in my path who would put me down—but not to pay any attention to them, they were simply jealous. Whether that was true or not, her support meant everything to me and gave me the confidence to cope with people's judgment along the way.

As a child, I loved to make believe. I remember I had a fascination with Native American people at a young age. It was my favorite role to play in pretend. I admired anyone who remotely resembled an Indian. My youngest aunt and my mom's best friend both had black hair that I thought was so beautiful. When I was only four, I used to tell them both how pretty their hair was and how I wished I had hair just like theirs. I made my aunt play Indians with me, we would put our hair in braids. Later in childhood, my interest in the native people was exhibited in my first high school crush on one of the few native guys in my school.

I was an artist in high school. I got attention for my drawing, painting, and writing skills. I loved music, and I especially admired Jim Morrison and Mick Jagger. The Rolling Stones and The Doors were groups from my parents' era, but I felt the music of the eighties, my generation, lacked depth. So I listened to classic rock. I drew pictures of Jim and read all his poetry and pondered it. Since he so greatly influenced me, I looked further into the poets and philosophers that influenced him.

In school, I didn't bond with the mainstream. I had a general disdain for authority and the social structure that supported Darwinism. I didn't like how the disenfranchised were treated, and I stood up for causes embodied by those that refused to, or couldn't, conform. I felt the culture of school was too caveman for me. I called the masses 'sheeple'. I also never felt subordinate to anyone. This made me a good communicator with adults: I felt that I was their equal, no matter their rank or supposed importance. I got an internship with the local newspaper and learned how to put my artistic skills together as a graphic artist. The adults I worked with gave me lots of encouragement and introduced me to many opportunities.

The working world was kind to me. I was offered a position as a graphic artist at the local newspaper that would normally have been given to a college grad. I appreciated the confidence I was given around the office. If someone needed help in anything, they would have me do it. I wrote articles, I did sales calls, I designed ads. The trust and support I was given gave me the confidence to achieve. I remember Vern told me that one the biggest things that attracted him to me was my commanding presence and my authoritative way of speaking at such a young age. He said, "You could converse on any topic and you spoke your mind." Of course he couldn't leave it as an amazing compliment. He then likened me to the powerful but seemingly unscrupulous women in the soap operas of the time. In fact, I admired him for that very same thing, but I didn't see it in me at all.

I met Vern the year before I graduated from high school, his stepfather, Mike, grew up with my parents so Vern's family visited Minnesota every few years. That visit was one I remembered because it was love and teenage angst at first sight between Vern and me.

The small town I grew up in couldn't contain me. I was a dreamer. I left for Los Angeles with my best friend, Robin, the minute I graduated from high school. We were invited to stay with Vern's family, and we gladly accepted and headed west with heads full of dreams.

Upon my arrival to Vern's residence in Los Angeles, Vern was still in high school and was going to prom with some little girl. I was secretly jealous, so I teased him about how cute he looked, asking if he bought his date a corsage and a pack of bubble gum. I followed up by asking him if he needed a ride or if he would pick her up on his bicycle. He burned a look right through me, laughed, and said, "You don't have any worries," seeing through my unprovoked attack.

Robin and I had a great time that year in California. I worked at a music store with lots of young people, and Robin had made friends with all the neighborhood kids our age. We were party central, just like college, minus the education. Vern's parents kept him on a tight leash. He was not to stop by after school, so when he did it was only for 10-15 minutes. They rightfully suspected that there was nothing good for a 15-year-old to be participating in at our place. However, that would not deter us. Family activities provided plenty of time for us to be alone.

I loved Vern's family. They were tight-knit group, and played together with new activities all the time. Every weekend was an adventure. I had never met anyone like Vern. He was good at everything. He was athletic, a runner in school, and also artistic, which I had prejudged as not possible since jocks were focused on the body and not on the heart and mind. He loved art and would ponder the meaning of a painting, or a sculpture, or a poem. He loved deep movies, even in his teens. While I loved The Big Easy, he appreciated A Room With A View.

He was also so charismatic, a great communicator who did large-group public speaking when he was only 13 years old. He was a leader in the community, a sheriff's explorer, on the student council, and much more. I couldn't believe someone so young was so competent and confident. The quality I enjoyed the most was how he could relate to anyone. Vern was genuinely kind and super funny with a sarcastic twist about him. He understood irony. At school he was liked by everyone...jocks, freaks, geeks, you name it. Normally I would discount such a popular guy, but he wasn't like most popular guys.

We had so many good times together. There was a camping trip that stood out for me. Vern and I went for a walk on the beach together. I remember enjoying the sensation of the sand slipping out from underneath my feet and hearing the ocean waves. I was new to the ocean, having come from the Midwest. Vern liked showing me all the wonders of California.

After playing in the ocean, Vern gave me a piggy-back ride. We walked over to a private spot under the boardwalk, and he spun me around till I flew off his back and he lost his balance and fell on top of me. He stroked my hair and my hand, but he didn't kiss me. To me, this exchange was better, and more intimate, than the first and only time I had sex to this point. Vern and I had such a great talk. We shared our hopes and dreams and inferred a life together (but of course we did not directly plan a life together, that would put our hearts at risk). I was going to become a film director. He wanted to be a CEO of his own business. We talked about a house we wanted to get, one of those modern houses with 18 foot ceilings, all glass windows on one side, and art hanging on the walls of the other sides. I asked him what kind of car he was going to drive and he said he would have a Cadillac, a Mercedes, and a truck. I told him I would buy him an El Dorado with the proceeds of my first movie. I was putty in his hands. I wanted him to have everything he could ever want, I adored him so much.

Making ends meet in Los Angeles in the mid 80's was not easy. LA was booming, and everyone was moving to California. Nine months after I arrived, I found myself having to do an about-face. I experienced my first failure when Robin and I couldn't afford our expenses. I had to head back home to Minnesota. I promised Vern I would be back after college. Surely I could get a better paying job with a college degree.

Vern and I were very frustrated by the confines of his age. He could not do the same things I was doing socially, and he felt especially restricted because he had parents to answer to. I remember my last day in LA; I felt I was being sentenced to prison. I cried so hard because Vern made me feel like I was abandoning him. We had become so close, and we shared dreams of a grand life together. Our friendship was so much deeper than the typical teenage relationship because the age difference kept us from a sexual relationship. As a consequence, we were forced to build on our friendship; it was more than hormones and lust.

One of the neighborhood kids who Robin and I were friends with, Michael, came back to Minnesota with us, or shall we say, escaped the law. He was in trouble at 17 for throwing a rock at a cop and was afraid he would go to jail. Back then we didn't understand the seriousness of Michael's alleged crime. All we knew was we liked having Michael around; he was a guy to protect us. He was the life of the party with that outgoing California style. This wasn't the most responsible period of my life. We were all college students, less interested in studies and more interested celebrating youthful exuberance.

Michael and I had a little too much to drink one night and ended up having sex, and—guess what—I got pregnant. The old adage, 'it only takes once' is true. It was only my second time ever having sex. Out of that one-night liaison, that impulsive act, came my beautiful daughter, Alycia. Michael was not in love with me, and I was not in love with him. We were two friends who had over-stepped boundaries. I decided to keep the baby, Michael decided to leave and stay out of my life.

I dreaded telling Vern the news and admitting what had happened...he would probably never forgive me. I feared the future I had planned with him, now, would never be. When I told him what happened, he was clearly shocked and disappointed, but he did not show how hurt he actually was. He would only share his devastation years later. That night, though, he made a joke of the situation and said, "So you slept with the town man-whore, and now you are pregnant. What did you think would happen?"

Vern came to visit me the summer after Alycia was born. Vern did not fixate on feeling betrayed. I explained that the pregnancy was achieved in a lapse of judgment, and that there was no contest to my affection.

That summer, we had a sweet romance. He had grown up quite a bit, he swept me off my feet with the confidence of a man. When Vern arrived in town, he came over unexpectedly. I was at my parents' house on the phone.

He knocked on the door, and I motioned him in. He was all by himself. I tried to quickly get off the phone and wrap up plans so I could greet my unexpected guest.

Vern was feeling very impatient and looked at me as if I were rude for keeping him waiting for even a minute. He took the phone out of my hand and said, "She'll call you back". He threw the phone on the floor, grabbed my arm, pulled me up close, and leaned in to put his beautiful, full lips on mine.

Whoa! Was I surprised. This was the moment I had been waiting for, Vern to sweep me off my feet. It literally took my breath away. I audibly sighed with pleasure. He then lifted me up and carried me away like in a Hollywood movie to the bedroom where we made love for the first time.

The end of the summer came too soon. The reality of our separate lives would soon be imposed. Vern said he wasn't sure if things would go the way we planned prior to me leaving LA the year before. He pointed out that a baby needs lots of support. I hid my deep devastation. Inside, I had hopes he would accept me for my mistake and we could continue with the plans we had made. Instead, we kissed goodbye, and that would be our last kiss in a romantic way for many years.

I had to grow up fast; I was now a single mom. My girl grew up surrounded by the same loving crew I grew up with. Alycia was my Dad's princess. She had him wrapped around her finger, to the surprise of us kids. My brother, Don, and younger sister, Carrie, still lived at home during Alycia's first year. Baby Alycia was my little shadow. She used to follow me around and say wonderful things like, "Mom, I just love being with you so much". She was a momma's girl, too. She would teach momma so much along the way.

When Vern finally graduated from high school, he went to the local private college. He became the vice president of the Latino club, stirred up controversy on campus, challenged the status quo, defended the underdog, and was adored and lusted after by all.

Vern and I religiously wrote letters and talked on the phone bi-monthly. A long distance call was still expensive in those days, so we had to be mindful. We no longer talked about being together, though I held out hope.

We had transformed our relationship into the best of friends, even though I wanted much more from him. We agreed to look at the possibility after he was done with college and firmly into his career. He did not want to put up expectations and be disappointed again. Though he genuinely connected to Alycia, the possibility of being responsible for another human being in the near future was something he was not ready for. After all, he was just beginning to claim some independence from his primordial family.

The summer before Vern started college, his mom let me in on a newly discovered secret that she assumed I knew. She told me she met Vern's boyfriend in a most shocking way. I tucked in my dismay just the way I imagined Vern did when I called him two years prior with the news I was pregnant. I pretended I knew about it and gave my condolences to Henri for finding out in such an unexpected way.

I collected myself and called Vern up the next day. I told him how his mom had shared what had happened last month. I asked him why, if we were best friends, didn't he tell me he was in a relationship, much less one with a man? I asked if what he felt with me was true, or if I was just an experience leading to his true feelings. After a bit of silence on the line he said, "I don't know. I always thought we would end up together so the in-between probably didn't matter."

I couldn't pretend anymore, and I started to cry, which made him cry too. I promised him that there would be no more secrets between us and at the very least, until the in-between was over, "Let's not hide anything, especially from one another." At least the honesty and acceptance between us could protect our bond.

I started dating after I realized there may not be a future for Vern and me. I met my first husband, Ed, at my job at the age of 23. I did my best to move forward, but Vern and I continued to support one another as friends. We visited at least once a year, which would always be loaded with fun. Vern would make me laugh. He would take me on adventures and we would always try something new together—new foods, new culture, new art, new music. My love, Vern, showed me his world and I shared mine. He was my guardian, and I was his.

After a couple years together, Ed and I moved to Hawaii. Ed's friend gave me a lead on a job, which I landed. Ed and I had a really life-enriching four years on the island. Vern was in a serious relationship. He built a business, bought and sold real estate, and he was involved with the city council and active in the business planning commission. He was receiving honors with the city and was elected vice president of the Latino chamber of commerce for Los Angeles. Vern invited me to a few of his major award ceremonies which I flew in for. When I came to town, we didn't spend a day apart. We were all about each other. With the exception of crossing any sexual boundaries, we acted like a married couple. Our partners weren't exactly comfortable with it, but they had to tolerate it, as it wasn't optional.

I received my first nod to the mystical in Hawaii. I met a woman through a friend of none other than Vern's family. This woman, Ivy Olson, was amazing, and I knew it instantly when I met her. Ivy Olson was selected as one of President Bush's 'thousand points of light' because she ran an organization that helped homeless families get back on their feet. She called it Angel Network, conceiving of it after she experienced a real Angel.

Ivy found herself starting over at a young age, raising two children alone and penniless. It was Thanksgiving, but she had just enough bread to feed her kids. So she made them a sandwich and took them to the park. She went hungry as they ate. A nice elderly woman came and sat next to Ivy and asked for her story. When the woman found out they had no one to celebrate Thanksgiving with, she insisted that Ivy and her kids come over that night for a dinner she would prepare.

Ivy, very appreciative, graciously accepted the invite. She and her kids enjoyed a feast and laughter with this woman. After a wonderful evening, Ivy thanked her and returned home. Ivy went back a few weeks later to return tupperware she used to take home left overs and, to thank her again for her kindness. She noticed her luck had changed coincidently with the meeting of this amazing women as she also landed a job that following week. She knocked on the lady's apartment door and got no answer. She knocked on the window and could see that there was no furniture in the apartments. Startled by the thought that something may have happened to her, she tracked down the landlord to inquire where the tenant had gone. The landlord said the apartment has been vacant for more than a month...

At that moment, Ivy knew she had been touched by an angel. This set her on her mission of helping others, a blessing that led her to form Angel Network for which she was awarded recognition from both President Bush and President Clinton. Evidently her story was also covered on the TV show called Touched By An Angel. I did not know any of this at the time I served on the board. But I did know she was an earth angel the minute I met her.

So, ultimately, it was Vern's family who got me involved with this magical lady and her organization.

On New Year's Day of 1997, Ed and I conceived my second child, Gabrielle. Just prior to her birth, we moved back to Minnesota to share our fortune with the clan. Gabrielle was a perfect baby—she barely cried and was happy all the time. Of course, all parents think their children are brilliant and beautiful, but Gabby really is and was. Gabrielle was Daddy's girl.

Ed was an incredible father and still is. Unfortunately, our passion faded over time. We started to really struggle to be happy together. Truth be known, I don't think anyone stood a chance. At some level, I was still holding a torch for Vern. Ed and I decided to split when Gabby was only three. I was so disappointed in myself and felt like a failure in every way. My life was an utter mess—marriage falling apart, kids hurting because of it, job going out of business, a speeding ticket that resulted in me having to go to jail for sassing the police officer—this was a definite low time for me.

Thankfully, Vern, my constant supporter was there to pick me up. When things were bad, he told me it wasn't because of my shortcomings, at least not long term anyway. He cheered me on and offered to let me start over at his place. He had bought this incredible, historical home in Pomona the year prior. He, too, had just gone through a break up and a business down turn. We were both experiencing loss and transition. I moved into his home for six months.

I remember a night during that time when Vern asked me to sleep with him in his room. He said he couldn't sleep and needed the person he knew loved him most to be near him. I hopped in bed with him as his good friend. I stroked his hair. He grabbed my hand and tenderly kissed it, my emotions rose up, and a tear streamed down my face and his too. I said, "What's wrong?" And he shook his head and said, "shhh." We held each other all night and when the morning came, we returned to the normal denial. I now wonder if only we had spoken and come to an understanding, would we have set a different fate in motion?

Vern was living the single playboy life to dull the pain, joking that when he was done having fun, we could finally be together and make a family. He told me I made the most beautiful children. His crass comment—not unlike the dozens I had made—really hurt me this time. I took a job opportunity in the San Francisco Bay and it appeared, once again, time was not on my side.

I moved to San Francisco. It was a beautiful city, and I had a great job, but I spent two years in hell and four years in purgatory and stagnation without Vern in my life. It seemed every time Vern and I were apart, I made bad decisions that hurt me. I hooked up with a man that turned out not to be good for me or my family. He was an alcoholic and everything that came with that. Vern was the first to see it, and warned me about it. I did not want to see it.

Of course, when everything broke down, when I broke down, Vern was the first to come to my rescue, even though I hadn't heard from him in ages. I picked up the phone, shattered by all my bad decisions in those couple years. I was sobbing at the mess that I'd made. Vern said, "Please don't cry, I will be up as soon as I can." And five hours later, he was there, holding me, making me feel simply human for my errors. "Hey," he said as he softly stroked my hair and held me, "You wanted to believe your love could make someone better, and it has. Just not that man."

After Vern left, he sent me a framed picture of him with a note that read, "Wherever you go, I will always be with you." I tried to call him to thank him for everything. I left several messages with no return call. I barely heard a word from Vern during this time, so how did he know to pick up that emergency call that night?

Vern and I talked only a few other times in the next few years. It turned out he was suffering even more than I was. He went from being a well respected businessman and community leader to a drug addict. I was unaware until I received a call from his mom asking me not to bail him out of jail. She broke down and told me about the hell she had been going through with Vern and said jail would be the only place that could keep him from killing himself for the time being.

She needed court help to compel him to attend treatment. He was addicted to drugs and had been in and out of hospitals. I had been completely unaware. Vern was hurting so badly but did not share a thing. He was always there for me, and yet, I wasn't there for him in his darkest hours. I felt terrible. I tracked him down and let him know I would be there for him like he was for me. I visited him in rehab and kept in much closer contact.

My friend Blake, who I knew from Hawaii and had been introduced to by a friend of Vern's mom, moved in to my place. The last time I saw Blake, he was only a boy. He was now a young man at age 22. Blake was an important actor on my stage. Though never a boyfriend, we had a deep admiration and love for one another. He was a great artist, writer, and musician with an angelic face like Kurt Cobain. Talented like him too. He honored me by telling me my interests in the arts inspired him as a teenager, which meant, in a way, that I was a muse: a most honored position. As an added value, when Blake moved in, Vern finally admitted feeling jealous when I sent pictures of us to him after he prompted me by sending pictures of him and his date.

Email From: Darcy Bellows
To: Vern Mascorro
Date: Mon, Sep 3, 2006 04:18 PM
Subject: Our trip

Hey, I enjoyed your fishing trip pics. Here are some pics from Blake and my trip to Sausalito.

Cheers, Darcy

On Sep 3, 2006 6:31 PM, Vern Mascorro wrote:

I hate him! I hate him! I HATE HIM!!!!!!!!!!!!!!!!

I hope he dies!

Tell him to find his own friend...Doesn't he know you're taken already...Really some faggots are just so stupid.

On Sep 4, 2006 07:34 PM, Darcy Bellows wrote:

You haven't done a good enough job of staking your claim! Seriously, NO one could take your place.

This is young Blake, you remember him ...he's all grown up... woohoo!

On Sep 4, 2006 9:25 AM, Vern Mascorro wrote:

Would you like me to pee on you...........then would he know!

On Sep 4, 2006 01:14 PM, Darcy Bellows wrote:

I can think of a lot sexier, more romantic ways.

Sep 4, 2006 2:25 PM, Vern Mascorro wrote:

Well, then tell me how? You are older and wiser than me.

I loved Vern's childlike response, he was so funny. Children can be honest, and honesty is disarming. I believe me getting so close to the young, handsome Blake finally motivated Vern to go for it with me. He reintroduced the idea of us, which also coincided with his sobriety.

When I told Vern that Blake and I were going to Europe together, he was not happy. He said I was being ridiculous, traveling with a boy, and demanded to know what I hoped to gain from it. I said I was looking to have a magical experience and a great time, pure and simple. That pissed him off even more, he told me to "grow up"!

While I was in Europe, Vern got into a horrible accident on a four-wheeler. He broke his back in two places. Doctors told him he may never walk again and recommended surgery. Vern refused the surgery; he believed the body could heal itself. He said no to pain killers so he could adjust his back in response to the body's message of pain, which he said was the key. Vern was walking less than a month later. When Vern was able to follow his own instincts and heal himself, he started feeling like Vern again. He regained confidence, and, after so much loss, he saw his potential again.

In May, 2007, Vern finally closed the business that was dragging him down, and moved in with me. He had graduated from his third rehab and was ready to start again. I had a stable job and a nice home. While the girls were experiencing typical challenges and successes of life for their age, I was feeling stagnant. I remembered a quote about stagnation being death, and I felt stuck. So I welcomed him with open arms.

Vern coming back into my life gave me a new lease on life. I felt like a giddy teenager. My dream since I was 17 was finally being realized. Vern and I would finally be together in a romantic way. We had a no-holds-barred romantic life. Vern awoke every sense and made me feel so alive every day. It was the best of all worlds. We felt we knew each other better than anyone on earth and had a deep trust and love that was indeed extraordinary.

CHAPTER 2: THE END OF THE WORLD AS WE KNOW IT

That day, the day of my peril, I was worried about work. We were in the middle of the worst recession since the great depression. The office climate was getting ugly. People were whispering about the banks shutting down cash flow to our company, which was causing panic that the business was going under.

I knew I could count on my man to get me through hard times just as he had for the last 24 years. My man always made me feel so special and protected. I knew I would push all of my worries out of my mind as soon as I saw him that night. I had his love to lift me up. My very last communication from him echoed how he supported me—this was truly the secret to our long-lasting love. We never lost our dedication and passionate focus on one another.

____

On Oct 30, 2008, at 11:05 AM, Vern Mascorro wrote:

Darcy My Love,

Never allow any man/woman to degrade you nor try to bring you to their level. I have heard your words of unhappiness with the current situation at work. I wish I could change your unhappiness. I do. I will work on understanding all you bring forward in order to better translate it to my family's business.

I Love You Bellows,
MASCORRO

____

That night, I silently rode home sensing the doom about to be laid at my feet. I knew something was wrong. I didn't hear from my man the rest of the day. We were supposed to have lunch. I called his cell, I called home, I emailed. No response.

As I arrived home, I received a call from someone at the insurance company; no details just an urgent order, "Get to the hospital now! Vern was in an accident." When I arrived, they said he wasn't there. It took them over an hour to locate him. My heart was racing with anxiety. The doctor finally came out, and her demeanor said it all.

"Do you have an update on Vern?" I asked.

"Please come this way," the doctor said.

"No, I don't want to come this way.

Tell me now!"

She just moved forward. "Have a seat. I am sorry to tell you, Vern didn't make it; we tried everything."

My voice escalated with irritation and disbelief. A wave of anxiety and shortness of breath overtook me.

"What? Back up! Make what? Where is he?

What happened?"

"He was in a very bad motorcycle accident."

"What? My man doesn't have a motorcycle!" I felt a second of hope; maybe someone had stolen his ID. "Are you sure the man matches Vern's ID?"

"Yes, he matches the ID," said the doctor.

"But, he doesn't know anyone here yet; we just moved here. There is no way he borrowed a motorcycle."

"I don't know," the doctor said. "The paramedic said it was a motorcycle accident, but maybe that was because his injuries were so severe it seemed like a motorcycle accident."

"Oh My God, no! No! NO!" I screamed.

I doubled over in pain.

There were a few moments where I gasped for air and sobbed before I felt myself shut down and my body take over, like protection mode.

Numbness floated over me. Everything slowed down. I heard the noises around me as if I were no longer present in the room. The air felt thinner, lighter. I felt a feeling of disassociation, the feeling of being outside looking in.

The doctor went into the technical details of the injuries, which I could not absorb. I had to call Henri, his mom, back. She was waiting. It had only been a few minutes, but I knew those few minutes were like endless hours.

Vern and his mom were as close as a mother and son could be. How was I supposed to tell a mother that her son, the son she spoke with every day, wouldn't be calling again? Those moments are too painful to retrace. I can only say it is not something you wish anyone to experience.

The days that followed were like a surreal nightmare. I was still in a state of shock as the family gathered to help with the business realities of death.

I didn't even know how to announce the tragedy to friends who were not close to the family, so I did it through email. I couldn't speak to anyone; the shock, the reality were too heavy to carry. I felt too sad to speak.

____

Email from Darcy Bellows: Date: Wed, Nov 5, 2008

Friends,

I can't pick up the phone yet, so I apologize for not having the strength. My fiancé, Vern, died last Thursday in a horrific accident. Many of you knew him, and some of you did not. I was so excited for you to meet him because he was such an incredible man.

If there is an afterlife, I will soon let you know because Vern had the type of spirit that he will find a way to give me a sign.

We will be celebrating Vern's life on Sunday Nov 10th on his family's reservation, Morongo, at 1pm.

Send me some strength to make it a celebration as he would wish.

I do not have everyone's email so pass it along to anyone that should know.

Thank You, We'll talk soon,
Darcy

———————

News briefs: The Fresno Bee: Oct 31, 2008 11:48 PM

Man killed in single-car accident is identified

The Fresno County Coroner's Office identified Friday the man who died Thursday in a car crash in northwest Clovis.

Vern Mascorro, 37, died as his car careened off the road and onto a bicycle trail.

The wreck happened on Willow Avenue north of Nees Avenue. Witnesses said the driver had bent sideways like he was reaching for something, and the car began drifting toward the curb while traveling about 50 mph. The driver never corrected his steering, and the car hit the curb and a street light.

The car carried the street light with it and smacked into the tunnel connecting the trail with the other side of the street.

CHAPTER 3: IN SEARCH OF...

Journal Entry Nov 4, 2008: Letter to Vern

Lover,

I remember the day I fell in love. You were just a boy in a man's body; you stood well above 6 feet at 14. Your beautiful tan-colored skin was in stark contrast to my own pasty white. In my part of the world, you were exotic and striking: part Native American, part Latino, your thick black hair, long black eyelashes, cut angular jaw, high cheek bones, full lips, dimples. Wow! You were stunning.

Your eyes contained a depth far beyond your years. When those beautiful eyes first met mine, my heart began to race. I thought to myself, "Look away, this boy has been met by many appreciative glances." I wasn't going to be another notch in your flirtation belt. I thought, "This kid has got to be so arrogant over his fortune in the genetic lottery."

Surprisingly, you looked away as quickly as I, as if to say shyly, "Were you looking at me?" Hmm, how perplexing? In my experience the few people I had met as lucky as you in the genetic lottery were so out of whack with their sense of self. I had devised a theory that God had a way of equalizing gifts—if given abundant physical beauty the person would lack depth, intelligence and compassion. Yes, my love, you were the catalyst to defy many of my preconceived notions.

I was talking to your mom, purposely avoiding giving you any attention. You stared right at me. I told her I had aspirations of moving to Venice Beach to become an artist, poet, writer, and filmmaker like Jim Morrison. You interjected some sarcasm something to the effect of "Oh! That's novel—Midwest girl goes to Hollywood to become famous."

"What!" I thought to myself, "You think you know me? Pretty boy thinks he's smart; he's got jokes." Or did I say it out loud? Your mom was shocked at your response to a girl you had never met.

She said, "Vern!"

That was the day you had my heart. I professed to you that I knew we would become fast friends; in fact, I believe I told you from that day forward you would be my "special" friend. I tortured you for your sarcasm by introducing you as my "special" friend to everyone we met. This became the foundation of our relationship. Indeed you were my most special friend; we would share our truths like no other.

That day I had met my match and my nemesis. If there's such a thing as a soul mate, you were surely mine. We enjoyed an amazing 24 year journey. We taught each other so much; you were the sun to my garden. You taught me the meaning of true love and life. I so miss that depth of experience. I barely know how to go on without you. Every minute ticks by so slowly as I await the day I can hear your soulful truth again.

Love Eternal, Darcy

A poem I wrote for Vern; email from Darcy Bellows to Vern Mascorro Feb 9, 2008, 2:41pm

Mascorro, you fulfilled my romantic notions of love.

Love equals...open eyes, open mind, open heart

refuge from uncertainty

soft comforting touch, a knowing glance

no longer wanting but full

a moment of pureness -- a child beaming with pride

feeling without doubt she is adored

free from expectation

free from disappointment

relief, rebirth, renew, the power of creation

cold and wet -- a warming ray of sun shine

forgiveness, redemption

harmony with imperfection

touched by grace of god - love of another

When I gave you this poem you wrote me such tender words. I truly knew I was loved. This type of heartfelt exchange between lovers is priceless, no measure of material wealth could ever compare. Thank you, my love; I never had to wonder if you loved me. Thank you for telling me so many ways every day. I never tired of it. Thank you for your writing. I will treasure it till I am returned to your protective arms; it will remind me how much I was truly adored.

Subject: your poem on love
February 9, 2008 8:48 AM Vern Mascorro wrote:

You have such a gift with words. I can recall when we were kids and I would love to read the letters you sent to me. I was proud to be loved by a person like you. Again, as a man, I share the pride you had placed so deeply into my spirit and my old torn soul. Your love has been the stitches that I needed to heal the torn, bloody heart I had made for myself. I can never thank you enough for always standing by my side. We have had a wonderful life together as friends. I am a proud man to tell all how you soon will be my wife.

Mascorro

Mascorro, for a moment I was touched by the grace of God with your love. I will most miss your soulful observations of each day. I bought this journal hoping you can read the letters to you from heaven, if there is a heaven...

Yours Always, Bellows

Like so many people in my generation, I felt spiritually anemic. Organized religion had let us down. We were a society of seekers, not satisfied with many of the answers. So many of the "answers" just didn't make sense. So many inhumane acts had been performed in the name of God. I had witnessed so many people perpetrating ugliness and judgment as if they were God, in the name of God.

I'd always been a hopeful agnostic. I didn't believe in what the MLM (multi-level marketing) pyramids, called churches, were selling, but I did believe in a God, something stronger and wiser that is a part of us. I believed in many of the teachings of the world religions; the ones that had no conflict of interest, no investment in becoming the ruling class or placing their breed above others. I knew buying membership came from man using God, not from God.

I believed in my hardworking ethical grandparents that worshiped in the big church. My parents didn't worship in the big church, but they did believe and practice the important teachings. They taught us the golden rule, which is simply to treat others as you would have them treat you. They taught us that we are responsible for our actions, and that sometimes we will make mistakes and it's important to learn from them. Most importantly they taught us that we would be loved no matter what. My human parents were pretty smart; imagine how wise God must be.

I did not seek to blame God for my horrific loss. I had realized long ago that once we left the Garden of Eden, the world was ours to experience, both good and bad. Many people wanted to make me feel like it was an act of God. The next few days of people offering their condolences and belief systems were rough. People say awful things when trying to avoid the heaviness of loss.

Here are things to avoid:

"One door closes, another one opens." My thoughts are, Oh joy I am so happy the segment of true happiness and fulfillment has closed. I can hardly wait to open the new door.

"We don't always understand God's will, but let me tell me you about the time he saved my loved one." You're not suggesting what I think you're suggesting.

"He will have it better in heaven." He had unconditional real love here. It will not be adequately replaced just as he won't adequately be replaced in my life.

"God's love is so much greater than we can imagine; he is now with God." What is my love, worthless?

"It's God's will." I refuse to believe it is God's will to harm any of his children.

"God works in mysterious ways." Not in my view. He gave us the keys to the castle when we walked out of the Garden of Eden. He gave us choice, no mystery, just an experience we asked for. It's called free will.

"Everything happens for a reason." No, in fact, often horrible things happen for no apparent reason at all, and many times these horrors go unnoticed by anyone at all. A child is not beaten or raped for a reason.

"It was his time to go." He went, so indeed it was, but you don't have to rub it in!

"I just lost my cat; I know just how you feel..." I wanted to say to each of them, "How could you think of God so dark and ugly? When I think God, I think peace, love and wisdom, not fear, control, and revenge."

My beliefs have always been different than those who believe God has personally scripted every minute of our lives. I cannot accept that his ego is so large he must be in control of everything. Who could believe he placed us here as pawns for his own amusement? We know a flawed human is one who insists on controlling others and his environment; why would we give God those flaws?

We have been told we have free will. You can't have pre-ordained destiny and free will running simultaneously. I refuse to believe God is an unjust, egotistical micro-manager, choosing who to let live and who to let die. How does he decide which innocent two year old child to save from a brutal rape and which to dispose of? I believe God to be much smarter and more compassionate than his children.

I think when someone is in heavy grief, all you should say is, "The person will be missed, and they were clearly loved." I see people on the online Widow Chat board hurt daily by others not knowing how to handle them. Some just keep their distance; others try to rush you to get over it. Sometimes distance works because the grieving feel no one on earth can relate to the emptiness, but other times we need a hand up. I found getting out of the house to focus on other things, if only for a moment, somewhat beneficial. I found anyone who wanted to talk about funny Vern stories comforting.

CHAPTER 4: OPENING DOOR NUMBER ONE

Though others' views were interesting, I needed to develop my own on this all-important matter. Others' opinions on the Why or Where Vern is now issue did not really resonate with me. I was driven to find answers for myself. Indeed, if there is an afterlife, if our energy and memories transcend our body's death, I would find him and he would find me. I needed evidence! Having been raised Catholic, I knew the Christian beliefs. So, I started reading material on every other belief system, researching on the internet day and night.

I started by searching for young widow support. I found the book Widowed Too Soon by Laura Hirsch. It's about a young woman's search for answers and her healing process. I found the description very similar to the position I found myself in, so I read more. On her website, she had links to mediums, and she noted one as being the best (this one, in her words, "changed her life"). Her name was Vickie Gay.

I clicked the link, even though I felt foolish. I visited the site, but it took me a couple of days before I finally called. I skeptically asked her about the process. She explained that she believed in God, that all gods are one God, and that she had a spirit room where she made connections to spirits. The room was adorned with symbology from all belief systems. Her philosophy on religion seemed agnostic and was not unlike mine. It felt like I had made the right call. She said that she herself was one quarter Apache. Shivers went up my spine; my man was one quarter Apache. I said to her, "I am looking for someone who is Apache."

She then replied, "STOP! Don't tell me a thing! Any medium that asks many questions is not a good medium. Don't tell me anything; it will interfere with my ability to receive. I will receive information from spirits and you will just verify that it makes sense. Do not elaborate; a simple yes to keep it going is fine."

With this advice, I decided to proceed with a reading. She sounded legitimate with the statements made thus far. This reading was only two weeks after the day he passed. I went in skeptical and would not accept ambiguous statements, but in my heart I felt confident that if this skill was real, then Vern would come through loud and clear.

Inside my head I was split. I was thinking, "Vern, if this is something that can be done I know you will come through. If this is just a scam like it often seems to be on TV, I won't be scammed twice."

The following is an unedited transcript of the phone reading with medium Vickie Gay.

First medium reading with Vickie Gay Nov 13, 2008.

VG=Vickie Gay, the psychic medium; D= Me, Darcy, the author and sitter, or the recipient of the reading.

VG: "Darcy, I need to say a prayer of protection. Visualize white light going around you. During the entire reading I need your feet not crossed and your arms not crossed. I need you open for me."

D: "Okay."

VG: "Just relax and let it happen."

D: "Okay."

VG: "You can interrupt and ask questions as we go, Darcy, you can ask any kind of questions, but wait 'till we get connected."

D: "Okay."

VG: "All right, you ready?"

D: "Yes."

VG: "Today is Nov 13, 2008 and this sitting is for--- can you state your name for the recording?"

D: "Darcy Bellows"

VG: "Okay, Darcy, here we go, I ask for a white light of protection. I ask for white light protection against all evil and negativity. Wrap the white light all the way around you. I ask for the highest and best spirits to come for you now. Okay, Darcy, I felt some energy came from left to right...no from right to left. I felt like this is my spirit control, which is going to usher in anyone that is going to come through."

D: "Okay."

VG: "I see a tall palm tree, and I see winds, and I see rain. And the palm tree is going all over the place, and I feel that is a representation of you."

D: "Hmmm"

VG: "You know how you see a palm tree and it so thin and so tall and it's being thrown all so badly... you feel that... 'my God, how does it withstand?' I feel this is you."

D: "Um-hmm"

VG: "You also look like your head is split. You're very open, your head is wide open and ah, you're just all over the place. You're split. You're like, 'Help!' I am seeing a bird fly off to the right of you. And I am hearing something about the north and now I am seeing a male's hand embracing your hand, holding it and placing it up to his chest. He holds your hand over his heart."

D: (I sigh heavily and try to hold back my tears.)

VG: "You are looking up to this person, so it must be their eyes are higher up than yours. At first I felt like he was trying to explain and then afterwards you are looking at each other. I see him stand very straight, but his head is tilted down to look at you."

Evidence review:

This opening statement to an outsider may have seemed general, but the gesture described between lovers just about dropped me to my knees in its significance. I instantly snapped back to one of the most important moments of my life.

Vern and I were standing face to face. We had just finished cleaning up after dinner. He grabbed one of my arms with both of his hands, his hands moved down my arm to my hand. I tilted my head and smiled. He moved my hand, cradled it, and placed it up to his chest. He flattened it out so I could feel his heart beating. He crossed his hand over mine, looked down at me, and smiled. "I wanted you to feel my heart beating," he said, a tear welling in his eye which instantly put my emotions on high alert. He relaxed his smile and said, "I love you as I have since the day I met you. If you want to marry, I do too, as there is no one else I would want to be with or to raise a family with. I did not know life could be this good."

I started to cry. I removed my hand and buried my head where my hand had been against his chest. I cried, and we laughed together. I said, "I am so glad you conceded to being my husband, I am such a lucky girl." He pulled my chin up to look at him. He winked and said, "Right you are."

Two weeks prior, we had a discussion after a wonderfully intimate entanglement. Lying in bed, we both were euphoric after a blissful session of lovemaking. Vern turned to me and said, "I want a baby". I replied, "I would love to have your baby, but first things first, we have to get married." I felt all girly and light hearted as I said it. He looked at me puzzled, "Why does some tradition that has not been sacred for decades in American culture matter or have any bearing on our ability to co-parent a child, that's silly."

I got a little more serious and said, "I don't care if it's meaningless to our society. I want your commitment to me before our family and our creator. We need to declare our devotion till death do us part."

Vern thought he had established his honor and intent with me, so he seemed puzzled over my statement. "I've waited 36 years to seed and have had many opportunities. The fact that I have not, and I have picked you to intentionally have a child with, says it all. Besides, I have been devoted to you in various forms for 22 years. Some certificate will not make that official."

I replied, "You're right, but it's a sacred ritual where we bring our families together, and it's symbolic of that ultimate commitment and devotion. It may be trivial to you, but to me it is not, and it will not be to our child. I am not going to be your baby factory. Just the fact that you picked me says nothing. I have two beautiful daughters with high intelligence and good personalities; maybe you're measuring my results and assessing the good gene pool. If you're looking for someone just to seed with, I suggest going much younger. That possibility is very open to you as you are, indeed, an Alpha male!"

I sprang up, irritated, and got dressed. I was upset with the fact that he thought the sanctity of marriage so trivial. It was obvious he had not even considered asking me to marry him. I remembered in the past he had given me a backhanded compliment when he was dating another woman. He said, "How come your kids aren't brats?"

In the first minute he described, through Vickie, the most significant moment of my life to prove it was him. He delivered and captured my attention like no other. I knew that was Vern. I snapped back to the present, and she continued.

D: "Where is he?"

VG: "He does not have his feet on the ground, so I don't know if he's telling me that he's in spirit or that he was not grounded. It's one or the other. When he was here, in the physical, he was not grounded because his feet are a little above the ground."

D: "Okay."

VG: "You need to know he is not dead; he is just in a different vibration. If he was dead, I could not talk to him. If he was at his final destination, I could not talk to him. You need to know that when people that cross over go into the spirit world, whatever it is that happens to them, they are not at their final destination. They are still growing, learning, evolving. When you allow this person to help you, he is helping himself. It's kind of like brownie points, or a merit system."

D: "Okay."

VG: "I don't think he has figured this out yet."

D: "Okay."

VG: "I get the number two with him, like two months, two days..."

D: "Two weeks."

VG: "He's been gone two weeks."

D: "Two weeks today"

VG: "He's giving me the number two, and he's not figured it out yet. That's what he was saying before that. He went to the light, so he is not stuck between the spirit world and here, which is good because then he can incorporate himself both here and there. He can do his learning and he can also be around you. And I see a big white fluffy dog, and I feel like when he saw this dog, he said, 'You're dead, and I'm following you'. And then I see a man, but that is what it all started with, a dog, and that was to let him know, 'Hey, come this way.'"

D: "What happened next?"

Evidence review:

Vern loved dogs, and he had at least a dozen of them in his lifetime. One of them was a big, cream-colored, fluffy chow he called Gorda. He loved dogs so much he was working on a service dogs' rights project before he passed.

VG: "Hold on...I got pounded into and I feel like I got three hits; they were all upper body right in the face and in the chest. I got hit more than one time. Whatever impact there was, another and another, there wasn't, like, one hit."

D: "Did he go instantly? Was he scared?"

VG: "He's telling me he had an out of body experience, so he flew out of his body before he even crossed over, and then he got back into his body, and it wasn't about being scared. It was like he didn't have time to do that."

D: "Right."

VG: "It was like something in motion."

D: "Yes."

VG: (Vickie starts to channel Vern.) "'And the only thing that kept going through my head was that everything is messed up. It was like going through my head over and over' (Vickie asserts) I see him looking down and he is sitting on the ground. His bottom is on the ground, his feet are planted on the floor. His knees are up, and he hangs his head down, and he is saying, 'Everything is messed up.' This is what is rolling around in his head.

He didn't think, 'I've been in an accident,' or 'ah, this is all happening to me.' He didn't think that he had crossed over; he felt everything was messed up; his flash of light was that everything got messed up. You know how some people say they see their life flash before them? That's not what happened with him; to him it was like everything was messed up because he had so much still to do.

So this man is, or was, not ready to cross over; he was not ready to go. Instead of seeing his whole life, it is more about what he has not done."

D: "Yes, that's how I feel too."

VG: "He gives you flowers; they all look white to me."

D: (I sob.)

VG: "It's the color you lost. He says they are all white; it looks like a bouquet to be held at a wedding that you lost."

D: "Yes, (I cry) we were to be married."

VG: "He said, 'Don't be angry, don't be upset, don't stomp on the bouquet.'"

D: "I would never do that."

VG: "No, it's just the different emotions. It's not being angry at him or at yourself; it's just anger at the whole thing."

D: "I do feel anger that he was taken away from me." (I weep.)

VG: "He has his hands on your shoulders. I just hear, 'I am so sorry.'"

D: "Oh!" (I cry.)

VG: "I don't feel like it was something he could have prevented."

D: "I know."

VG: "He said 'no matter how you danced around this whole thing—backwards, forwards, upside down—this one couldn't be prevented'."

D: "I know."

Evidence review:

The car accident was horrific. It had three major impacts, and the injuries were as described. I knew he would have fought to survive, and I knew he would have been in shock. He had previously survived two other accidents with super human healing powers. He had the will to survive in much murkier times, so I knew he would have fought this time. Vern had told me he was never so happy in his life, even with the conflict we were constantly working out.

The strange thing is, Vern also shared with me the month prior that he had a fear of dying in a car accident. I did not assume any precognitive ability. I thought having two prior near death accidents would have caused irrational thoughts for anyone. I wondered, if we had listened to the fear, could we have prevented his death? The words used were "messed up," and these are his words. This was truly shocking to all of us! We were finally right on track in our lives. We were planning our wedding, planning our child, finally getting into the flow. We had no way of knowing all of our dreams would be dashed in a second.

This was no phony making of generalizations. She was giving specific details that matched the police, doctor, and witness reports. I was elated and filled with sorrow, all at once. My lover's consciousness did not die. She did not even know my name prior to the reading. She wasn't looking at me to know my age. At this point in the game, there was nothing published on the web with my name on it affiliated with his. She did not have Vern's name. Actually, she didn't even know who I was looking for. So there was no Google wizard, looking up what happened as we spoke.

VG: "And he grows wings, so I know he's going to be your angel on the other side. So I know he's going to help you, because he shows me that. You need to know that he's just in another vibration. He's not dead."

D: "Will we be together again?"

VG: "You will have a very long life, but he is going to be right there when you go; I see you running into each other's arms. This person is the love of your life."

D: "Yes, he is."

VG: "The other people, the other relationships, are going to be…not to be alone and all that."

D: "Hmm."

VG: "But he is always going to be there to help. And whoever you're around or whoever you love and care about, he will help them too. Because he knows that if good things can happen to them, they will be shared with you. Bottom line, he's helping you, you're his interest."

Evidence review:

I believed this to be absolutely true. Vern stood by me in life as we both loved other people, when he was unavailable to me. Of course he would feel this way in death when he physically could not be there.

VG: "He wants to make you aware to talk to him; you don't talk aloud or write things down?"

D: "I do; I'm writing a journal."

VG: "That way, he knows exactly where you are coming from and what you want."

D: "So when I need help, he wants me to journal it."

VG: "Yes, because at that point you ask him. You've given him permission, and he can take it a step further. That way, he knows what you want, and he doesn't have to sift through all the pros and cons floating in your head. That way, he knows where to put you, the right place at the right time, otherwise, he just has to observe.

'I love you'."

D: "I love you too. I miss him so much."

VG: "Either you're fixing or he's fixing clothes for each other. That is what he is showing me. He is folding clothes and you, or he, did this over and over again for each other, and this was significant to him."

D: "Yes!"

Evidence review:

She was talking about the fact that Vern was doing laundry for me, putting my clothes away and organizing them. Every day of the last year of his life he folded and washed our family's clothes and put them away. This was actually very significant for both of us. Vern spent his adult life working outside of the home as a businessman; he did not do housework. He had a maid for the last ten years prior to our union.

I spent most of my life having to do everything for myself. I really appreciated someone managing the home. Having help meant so much to me. He brought order to chaos in the home. He had mentioned many times that he was shocked to find himself folding laundry. One time, in a fight, he told me I needed to back down. He said everything was happening so fast. He had gone from a businessman and a freewheeling bachelor to a stepdad doing laundry. This pointed out how significant that was to him.

I must say, he folded things perfectly. I never had the precision that he had. He made a perfect bed; he folded things squarely, without wrinkles. He also taught Gabrielle how to do laundry. His being a stepdad and teaching responsibility was huge for both of us.

D: "Have all of his wishes been honored as far as his celebration of life? I know one side of his family was questioning the choice of being cremated."

VG: "He's saying that when he left that body, he left it, and that it doesn't matter what they did with it."

D: "I know."

VG: "Whatever is done, he's not in that body anymore. The only thing he cares about, the most important thing, the highlight of his life, was right now, right before his passing. What was going on with him that was of most and utter importance, was you.

It wasn't some fight he had with his mom, or some wonderful or passionate project that he was building, or that he was so involved in heightening his career. His passion, his utmost interest, his thing, was you. And it was taking all that to the next level and that's where he was. He said your plans were on their way, and then he crossed over and it was a shock. It was fast. It was not painful because he had to get out of the body before he crossed over. And then he had to go back in. And then he crossed over and then couldn't get back in it.

Because if he hadn't crossed over, the body would not have been good. If they patched him all in pieces and put him back together, he would have been in a coma because he had gotten out.

So if there had been more advancement and Humpty Dumpty could have been put together again, it would not have been good."

Evidence review:

Vern and I had specifically talked about burial verses cremation because there was a quarrel in Vern's family surrounding cremation decisions. So Vern made his position clear to me, which matches the response.

The doctor said Vern had so much brain damage he would have been in a coma if his heart had survived. The most touching were the words and sentiments that said this was him. He told me with the exact words that our love, our life together, was the highlight of his life. It was mine too. He also said his sole focus for this year was us and building our home. These words were the exact words I needed to hear. I was overwrought with emotion.

D: "Right, I do know that...Can he give his mom comfort? Because she is not sleeping."

VG: "She keeps waking up with nightmares or thoughts of what did not happen. She is working out issues in her dreams. She needs to know that what she is dreaming about is not messages from him; they are ways her body is working out this nightmare. It's actually keeping her from sleeping because she does not want to have them. It would be a good idea for her to journalize her dreams so they don't repeat themselves. She can say 'I got it'. But he is not visiting that way yet; he will later. And it will be like a visit; it's very different than a dream. It will be like he had been there. He is telling you he is okay. 'I am just trying to figure things out. I have looked at that whole situation and know I couldn't have gotten out of it, no matter how I did it'."

D: "I know."

Evidence review:

Vern's mom told me she wasn't sleeping. She kept wondering if she could have made it to Fresno before he died, that maybe she could have helped save him. Henri had helped her son a few times come back from a near death experience. There were many things in her mind preventing her from sleep.

VG: "'Now I am just trying to figure out what to do next. The only thing I have is you. I feel that you are the only one that knows me; I think I was just for show.' He didn't let anyone in, so they really didn't know him; he showed a front. That was his personality. That was him. I don't know; it looks like that is what he did, so you are the only one that knew him."

D: (Sobbing) "Yes, I know."

Evidence review:

Since Vern was a boy, he confided in me. Our relationship, or feelings for one another, was initially a secret because he was 14 when I was 17 and then 18. We decided to delay our romantic entanglement until it did not have to be a secret. I was turning into an adult; he still had to ask to stay out after 10pm. That age difference was big back then. He told me over and over again that I was the only one he felt comfortable being himself with. He told me he felt like "a show," he felt he had many expectations to meet. The cornerstone of our relationship was this solid foundation of trust and honesty, a safe place to be in a sea of societal expectations. I encouraged Vern to be comfortable in his own skin, but he always feared disappointing others. So, the duality of his life was an ever-present issue that he slowly worked through during the last part of his life. This fact makes this part of the reading more identifiable and personal than anyone on the surface could assess.

VG: "I'm so sorry, he is standing there. He is putting his face up against yours. He is messing with your sleeve, and then I see a summer thing, a shirt, he is messing with the sleeve of that. I just feel very thin material. He likes it when you let your hair down. I think he is showing me your beauty. I think he is showing me how beautiful he feels you are."

Evidence review:

Just two summers before he died, when we came together as a couple, I remember him looking at me and saying he enjoyed my softer side when I let my hair down. He said it was something he hadn't seen before and was very sexy. In that moment I remember actually feeling sexy, secure, and so in love.

VG: "The only thing he keeps doing is going in circles about being at that the wrong place at the wrong time. Maybe it was the right place at the right time because he was supposed to leave. But he has been looking at the situation every which way, and he still keeps doing that. He keeps going in circles with that, about how he could have gotten out of it. He just doesn't see how it could have been altered...that puzzle, no matter how you put it together, the results end up the same."

D: "I know. Is he safe now?"

VG: "I want to see if this man will go to the light. I want to make sure…for sure because he keeps going in circles, and he should show me other stuff.

How did you address him when he was here, not his birth name but what did you call him when he was here? I want to call his vibration."

D: "Mascorro, his last name Mascorro."

VG: "You called him Mascorro?"

D: "Yes."

VG: "Say it with me 3 times. Say it with me. Ready, go, Mascorro, Mascorro, Mascorro.

I feel high energy with him."

D: "Yes."

VG: "He is not ready to cross over. He is talking about 28; he's giving us another number. He already gave us two weeks. The 28, I don't know what that 28 is."

D: "Don't know."

VG: "A date? Days? I see candles so it has to do with a birthday."

D: "Oh yeah, his mom's birthday was on the 28th, two days prior to his death."

VG: "He's puckering up like he's going to kiss. He's sending you kisses, and he's flipping a book, he's flipping through the pages of a book. It's a hardback. There are not a lot of pages in it."

D: "Is it my journal I am writing to him? I only have a few pages written to him so far."

VG: "I don't know, that is just what I am seeing."

D: "I bought a leather-bound journal."

VG: "Okay that's probably it, and he's puckering up again, and I see him behind your shoulders. So he's like, observing what you're doing."

'Talk to me, talk to me, talk to me'." (She gets emotional when she says this for Vern.)

D: (I cry.)

VG: "'I am just as lonely as you are, and I have to figure it out over here too. I need your helping hand and I will give you mine'."

D: (I weep.) "Okay. If I talk, does he hear me?"

VG: "'You sound very distorted, but I am working on it,' and he said through this communication with him, I have introduced him to a bunch of spirits that are going to help him out so that he can hear you better.

He asks that you try to have a lot of plants and flowers around you. That way he can see their energy and know where you are as you move around."

D: "Okay."

VG: "When you pass by them, he will see that energy and know that you are there. He can't see you, but he has a sense of you, like a feeling. He's having the same feelings as you are, but he says he'll progress, that he's a quick study."

D: "Yes."

VG: "And that he's pretty witty, so he's going to figure it out. And he's talking about some of my friends in spirit. He's going to talk to them and figure it out, he said. He is not going to leave you alone and says, 'I've lost the love of my life to time'."

D: "Yes!"

VG: "'And I feel displaced'."

D: "Yes."

VG: "'And I won't have it, I won't have it! I plan to help you all I can. I give you my hand... I give you myself'."

D: "Oh! Vern."

VG: "He's down on his knee.

Because he's trying to lower himself down to where he can look up at you."

D: "Aahhh!"(I cry!)

VG: "'I, I feel like you're my angel as well; I feel like you're the only one who ever really knew me.'"

D: "Yes." (I gasp.)

VG: "'And I am so sorry I had to leave you before our ceremony'. He shows me a vision of a ring just rolling on its side."

D: "Ahhhh" (I scream and cry.)

VG: "He keeps saying he's okay."

D: "Okay. Does he see any of his relatives that have passed? Does he see anybody there for him?"

VG: "I feel a man, and I feel a dog but he has not explored that area. He's been too busy with the ties that have to do with you."

D: "Yes."

VG: "He has not even gone to his mother...That's why he said these dreams are not visits, because he hasn't been anywhere. He's been very much around you. He says he's sorry because he's just been trying to help himself right now and then, yeah, he shows me the number two again. So, he hasn't been there very long."

D: "Right."

VG: "He said that before, 'So please understand, and my mom has got to understand it's not that I love her any less, I just have to get my stuff together'."

D: "Yes."

VG: "I see your hand and his hand reaching out to each other and I see a long wooden box, it looks a box of matches for the fireplace, those long ones, a case like that, a long container."

God, this guy likes to kiss you. He's puckering up to you again!"

D: (I mix crying and laughing.) "I like to kiss him too. The box is a wooden cigar box he kept his things in."

VG: "Do you have any questions? If he can't hear it, I will try and repeat it."

D: "So he's still figuring it out?"

VG: "He is going to be around. He's not going to leave your side. You're going to live a long, long life. There are going to be other relationships but they are not going to be 'the one'. They will be in your life so you will not be alone. But he knows that you know that he is the love of your life. The relationships will not be the same.

He will be helping you. He is going to figure out how, and you need to give him permission because he wants to put you in the right place at the right time. 'I am not dead, I am not dead, I am not dead'."

D: (I weep.) "Okay. Who does he want to have Princess?" (His dog.)

VG: "He's talking about somebody not being home enough?"

D: "Yes she is very lonely; she knows something's up."

VG: "I am seeing someone who is not an adult. It is a girl, not an adult?"

D: "Is she, like, 13? Vern's friend, Claridad, asked about her; she has a daughter who is a teen."

VG: Yes, or little younger. If she's 13, she's not fully developed yet. He knows what to do. He's already checked all that out."

D: "Oh okay."

Evidence review:

I later found out that Vern came to Claridad in a dream and asked her to take the dog.

VG: "He's puckered up again. He's funny, though, he puts his lips way out there."

D: (I laugh and remember a picture he sent me when I was on a trip with this exact image.)

VG: "You know so much about him that the family does not."

D: "Yes.

Do you have any messages for Alycia or Gabby?"

VG: "I just hear 'Daddy's going home'."

D: (I whimper.)

VG: "I don't know what that means, but that's what he said."

Evidence review:

These are Vern's stepchildren, my daughters, which the medium did not know. Vern took his role of stepdad/parent seriously. The minute he moved into our house, he treated them as his own.

VG: "'I just want you to know that I am here and that I am not going to leave your side.'"

D: "Okay, mm"

VG: "'I want you to know that I hear you. I hear you right now.'" (Her tone was sad and slowed and emotional.) "'And I have been by your side every single moment. I went to you the moment I crossed, and I was with you, pointing at myself. There is no one else I can be next to until I can figure this all out. I can't do any more. I cannot help mom, I cannot help anyone.'" (Her voice cracks a bit through this.) "'I can't help nobody, I gotta figure it out, I gotta see what to do next'."

(In her own voice.) "Did you go to the light? Did you go to the light?"

D: I say, "Yes go to the light. You can build our home for us there."

VG: "He shows that he's packing a few clothes. He's, like, packing a few clothes in a duffle bag and throwing them in the backseat of the car. I see the backseat of a car. I am happy go lucky, and everything is ok. He gets in the back seat, and you get in the driver's seat. He is trying to tell me he will be with you wherever you go."

D: "I can't stay in Fresno without him. There is no life here without him. Maybe that is what he is saying."

VG: "He is going to be with you no matter where you go. He is not where his ashes are. You need to know that whereever people's remains are put is not where they are. And, if you visit them, they have to go there too. They don't hang out there. Wherever you are is where he is.

The only thing is, right now, you need to be strong because he is going to put you at places where you and he went. Because he will be running through that so he will be taking you through that too. It will bring back memories. He is going to work all the issues out. But he is okay, he's just working it out.

He is okay; he needs to let you know that.

He says you worry about him, and you are still worried about him."

D: "Yes."

VG: "He is not in pain, he has left that body. Nothing is wrong with him, now he is sharp as he ever was. As far as his personality and who he is, that high energy power, he has still got it going on. He is the same there.

He just has to figure out how to do it without a body, tapping into this vibration. You are just vibrating in a different space.

'It's like you're out of town, but I am going to reach out to you. The whole separation that's been going on for years is changing, and I am ready to learn. I'm not going to just let the days go by; I am ready to learn. My life was so short. I just blinked my eyes and it was over. It was very short, precious and short'."

D: "Yes."

VG: "He is talking about how you made his life."

D: "He made mine too."

VG: "So, he saying it's like you are the highlight of his time here because he got to know the real expression of love. By what he is saying, I feel like he wasn't in love before, he didn't get to experience it until then. It was like you finally ran to each other."

D: (I cry.) "It took us 23 years to get together as a couple."

VG: "It's like I see two people standing together and you are pushed together, face to face.

He's got a lot in the works. You are going to be going along thinking all these miracles are happening, but they won't be miracles. It will be him working the natural laws. You have good things coming your way and he's going to manifest it."

D: "Oh!"

VG: "He's talking to various people in spirit. He is talking to people; I know he is trying to find out everything he can about connecting to here. There he can suck up everything. His head is very big, his brain capacity is very large. He's sharp, a quick learner. You're going to see a lot of progress. This connection is very good for him; he is getting to meet many people. I think right now he is pretty much just around a man and his dog. This dog reminds me of a Great Pyrenees or a big, white, long haired dog, a sheep dog or the dog that takes care of the sheep dog."

D: "Is that grandpa, Vern?"

VG: "I don't know. I feel it's an older man; I just see khakis. He just laughs. I asked him and he just laughs, I think he's tickled that we are even talking to them. The older man has to do with him not you. He's not your grandpa."

D: "Right."

VG: "He said that you tire...He gives me a pain on the inside of his knee, a throbbing pain. Oh he didn't make it go away, so I didn't hit it - he's supposed to make it go away. It's a throbbing pain the inside of the leg. When I get, it he's identifying something that has to do with you or him."

D: "Um, don't know...he was a runner, so he had incidental knee pain. My sister, Carrie, was having knee pain last week when she was out here. She was recently diagnosed with arthritis."

VG: "He's acknowledging it. He made it go away so you hit it.

He said 'I just want to be with you, I just want to be with you. You need to know I am not going to leave you alone, and I am going to help you. Talk to me, you can write in the journal, that's fine, but just talk to me'."

D: "Will he be able to read the journal and its letters to him?"

VG: "Yes, he sees all that. 'We were at our crossroads. We made a lot of people talk, didn't we?'"

D: (I laugh.) "Yes, we sure did."

VG: "'We were filled with drama; I just feel like a movie that's drama'."

D: (I chuckle with affirmation.) "There was never a dull moment."

VG: "'And I had fun with you! You need to know'."

D: "Me too."

VG: "'I was so shut down. I was so shut down, and it's like I finally opened up to somebody. Nobody knows me and nobody has known me for 20 years and I finally found someone to open up to and here I am, and it pisses me off'."

D: "I know. Me too." (I start crying.)

VG: "'But I am going to deal with this, and you know I always try to be the muscle. This time I can't muscle it, but I am going to figure it out and I am going to give you a helping hand and from what I understand when I am helping you I am helping myself so I am not quitting'."

D: "That's all I ever wanted was to be with him, and then we had it for a little bit and, like he said, we were at a crossroads and we were coming to a complete understanding, I felt."

VG: "'And then the rings roll around on the ground on their side and they don't end up on your fingers.'"

D: "Yes."

VG: "He's talking about traveling, flying, and I feel like Texas stuff. You know how you go to a Texas Roadhouse and the Texas stuff with a cowboy?"

D: "He was listening to country music?" (It didn't make sense.) "Gabby said he listened to country music before I got home at night."

VG: "Hmm, He's showing me.... you know, how you go to a Texas Roadhouse and they do the line dancing and Texas stuff. I saw travel, and then I saw the Texas stuff country music really loud and the line dancing. Have you been to the restaurant Texas Roadhouse?"

D: "No."

VG: "Nothing but country music. They serve up steaks, and they have peanut shells on the floor. They line dance between serving tables. You need to go there. And then I see an airplane but you need to go there."

D: "We will go there."

VG: "'I'll be there; it's part of the roller-coaster. You're doing happy stuff and finding me out, all the things I have revealed to you'.

He is showing me a horseshoe, you know the lucky horseshoe and (Vickie chuckles) he just made his voice real low. It sounds like he is mimicking a sheriff or something. I think he likes to play with you."

D: (I laugh.) "Okay, yes he did. It was the secret to our long-lasting love."

VG: "He was playful.

'I just wanna be me. I want you to know that I am here'.

That's why he is doing all that. I am hearing him in character. If I start talking in the first person it's him. I am just allowing as good of a connection as possible."

D: "Oh, I got that."

VG: "Did he have stomach problems or something because I feel like I barfed?"

D: "Yes, he took Tums every day."

VG: "'My right ear hurts. God, I physically miss you. I just want to hold you'."

D: "I do too!" (I cry.)

VG: "He was to the point that he wanted to give you everything."

D: "And his love is all I ever needed."

VG: "Not a lot of people understood him. 'And I am so happy that I had you even in my arms at all'."

D: "I feel that same blessing but I also feel anger for it being taken away. It was so short."

VG: "'You are going to have me for a lot longer than you think. I am going to watch out after you. I am going to bring you good luck'.

He is also doing a little dance because he's proud of himself that he is able to let me hear him. He is sending me vision and I am telling him it's what I do but he's saying, 'yeah but I have to send them'.

Oh, he likes to pat himself on the back for what he does. I guess this is just his personality showing through so that you know that it is him and he kinda squints his eyes when he was telling me that. Right now the candle is flickering like crazy, and I feel it has to do with him.

I need to talk to you and not focus on the candle so he stopped. He said, 'He's a wild one'."

D: "Yes! He is."

VG: "I heard it and then he said 'Say it. Say I am wild one', so I said it.

'I love you so much!'"

D: "I love you so much!"

VG: "He guided you to me."

D: "I did find you kind of magically."

VG: "Yep, he guided you to me."

VG: "He's the one that instigated all of this, and he would not leave you alone. He had you figured out and how to connect with you within an hour!

You must have been feeling him right away within the hour; he went to you the minute he crossed over. It was like 'look what happened' and he was going back and forth. He was on it.

He led you to a way to communicate with him, and he says to me 'and you're the one, you're the one...'

I appreciate that." (Vickie says this moving back to herself.)

"His voice, he is trying to manipulate my throat to make me talk the way that he would talk. I feel a tightening of the throat area, a lot squinting with him."

D: "Oh?"

VG: "'I feel so at peace now, talking to you I just feel so at peace now'."

D: "Thank you, I feel better too."

VG: "'It's just that I have been working so hard to get to you, and now I feel so at peace now that we know what to do. I will not leave you alone'.

He brought up a birthday earlier. It's somebody's birthday; he wants to acknowledge that.

He is going to be with you through the holidays, and it's going to be hard for you. Know that, but he will walk with you. He will be right there by your side. He will be turning the pages of your book. You need to know he is there, he is going to help you. He is not dead, just consider him your angel." (Voice is saddened)

D: (I woefully cry.)

VG: "'And you're mine! There, where you are, and I am so sorry this is not where I want to be'."

D: "No, I know...ohhh"

VG: "'It's all their fault'."

D: "Whose fault?"

VG: "He's talking about what happened to him. All of a sudden my face just felt uncontrollable muscles spasms in my mouth, cheeks and across there. He was like it was their fault. He's got some issues here to work out about the whole situation and his crossing. But you have to understand, he hasn't been over there that long. He is figuring out how to communicate to you, how to get from point a to b, but he is still going in circles with that whole thing that happened to him."

D: "Uh huh.

A witness said that he leaned over in the car, and yet another witness said he was slumped over."

VG: "I hear a loud scream, and it's male! And it's not like screaming words, it's…I just hear a scream."

D: (Sigh) "Don't be scared."

VG: "He's not scared. It's something sudden. Like shock. Yes, it's not fright. Just for a moment I got a pain on my neck."

D: "Hmm…the streetlight?"

VG: "I heard a creak in here. This man is not going to be with you only now. He will be with you for the rest of your life 'till you are back together again."

(The buzzer goes off to close the session.)

VG: "You need to give him some time. You have helped and done your part. He needs a little time to work things out. He knew the time was up, and he wanted to get that in before we were done. I will leave you with that."

D: "Thank you."

I needed undeniable proof, and it was delivered.

When I think about the evidence, it was the personal connection described that really struck me.

I actually had recent emails to support many of the statements.

Vern once told me that loving someone was easy, and that he loved many. But that more than loving me, he enjoyed me. When I first heard this I did not absorb it. I thought, 'you enjoy a puppy'. In hindsight, the statement made profound sense. You have to find someone you have fun with, not forced fun but fun just being, because one day the surge of hormones will taper and you will be left with what is. We had that. I didn't have to wait till the weekend to recharge; most every night was fun. I have loved and had fun occasions with many, but I now know what that means. We enjoyed each other's ways, our similarities and our contrasts, we found them fun.

Vern had lived many lives. He had many highs and lows. He had everything materially at a young age. He was an entrepreneur, a self-made man. Right before Vern had come to stay with me, he had fallen from grace. He had a five year period where he excommunicated himself from everyone, including me. He would call maybe two or three times a year. He had fallen into dark times after his business and relationship failed. One night we were talking about this period he had just survived. He spoke the exact words Vickie had just uttered. He said he was 'so shut down'. He had given up all hope of any kind of happiness. He said he could not believe his reversal of fortune when he found love with me again. He told me that my family, our love, brought him more happiness then he ever imagined possible. He told me he did not know life could be this good. I felt the same gratitude for this gift. Hence, the bitter awful irony of his life ending just after it was starting to get good.

____

From: Vern Mascorro
Subject: You (Darcy)
Date: Aug 5, 2008 10:42 AM
To: Darcy Bellows

Thank You............You are a WONDERFUL woman. I only came to life when the creator placed me in your life at a young age. I am who I am. I am proud of myself (today). It has taken me many years to type that. I am "Vern". I will try to do better for you. You are the sun in my life. You are the rose in my eyes. And you, Darcy, have and will continue to be my first and only true love.

MASCORRO

____

From: Vern Mascorro
Subject: Sharing
Date: Nov 23, 2007 11:00 AM
To: "Henri (Mother) Mascorro"

Hello Mother,

I want to share how nice my Thanksgiving was. This was the first time I spent a holiday as a father and husband to be. Never before have I felt so needed and loved. The emotion felt/feels nice. In my past world of blackness and sadness, Darcy and her family have brought me color and warmth. I am so quickly peeling off my layers of hurt and pain I have kept in my soul and spirit.

As smart as I believe or think I am, never before did I know or understand what it meant to connect with another kind soul such as Darcy. I now today know that only now has life begun for me. Only now have I been so touched by another person. Only now have I started to become the man I was made to be. I know and understand I have always had your love. But for the first time I am feeling another's true love towards me.

My life today, Mother, is so wonderful it is hard. In a positive way. For almost 6 (six) years, I kept myself from all and everything. I stayed in dark places and tried often to kill myself with Meth.

As you well know, my depression pulls me to the deepest of dark holes.... But with family like you and Darcy, I am always able to return to the bright wonderful world you both keep me in.

Vern

____

Journal Entry, Letter to Vern: Nov 14, 2008

Mascorro my love,

Where do I start? You always know what to say and what to do. How do I live without you by my side? You encapsulated our relationship, our feeling, with well-chosen words through a medium, in a way I cannot deny it was you. You said everything I needed to hear.

Through my tears I cry with relief that you found me. I cry with joy that your beautiful soul lives on. I cry with sorrow for myself, not knowing how I will go on without my trusted companion by my side, the one who always knew the right thing to say.

Our family, my sister, Carrie, and my nephew, Shane, listened together to the reading, and we all cried. We cried for the gift of being able to hear you once more. We cried for a lost life that brought such passion to our lives. You had that ability to incite excitement and passion for living. You lit up the room. You believed anything was possible, and you made me believe in that too.

Do you remember when we were in our twenties and we all played truth or dare with my family, and a bottle of crown royal, and a video camera? I remember you got everyone to spill their guts, but I don't actually remember you telling much at all!

Oh yeah, that's because you were fearless with the dares, run around the block naked, "okay, like that's some big deal"... you knew I would be more embarrassed than you would. So needless to say, I didn't put anything like that out there and certainly nothing you would find daring. You lived so fearlessly compared to most of us, yet inside you never saw it that way. You were "the wild one" just like you said. I think for the most part you got it—life is for love, creating, and enjoying.

Yours eternally,
Bellows

CHAPTER 5: HEALING THE SKEPTIC

I shared this miraculous reading with everyone who loved Vern. I recall my brother, whom we both loved dearly, giving me the skeptical "Hmm," as if to say, "My poor sister is hearing what she wants to hear, and someone took advantage of her grief." He gave the same "Hmm," that came from my father and my father in-law (to be).

I did not receive this concerning expression well from my brother. I said to him, "Who do you think you're talking to? I am not some doe who can be taken advantage of. Explain to me how a lady who only knew my first name, not my face, got that I was about to be married and that I lost the love of my life, that the death happened two weeks prior, and that it was his mother's birthday on the twenty-eighth. She gave a very detailed depiction of the accident and his injuries. She revealed things that were important to him but wouldn't be to others, like folding my clothes and doing my laundry after being a businessman workaholic. The last thing he thought he would be doing was the family laundry. Do you know, he did not even own a washer and dryer at the last home he owned? He sent everything out, and his cleaning lady picked it up and put it away. So doing laundry was huge!

Do you do your girlfriend's laundry? No, you don't! Did my father do his wife's laundry? No, no he didn't. This is unique and specific to us.

It even seems that this medium was not just reading my mind because there were a couple of areas in the reading that I could not place and were not in my memory. Brother, if this lady wasn't speaking to Vern, who was she speaking to? How did this happen, Don? Please explain it to me."

I was talking to my friend Dan from work about the reading, and the one puzzling thing that I couldn't immediately place came to light. It was about the Texas Roadhouse thing. Dan said, "Darcy, we were supposed to go to Logan's Roadhouse the weekend he died, a 'Texas roadhouse' with country music and a place where you can throw peanut shells on the floor. Darcy, don't you remember him talking about it the weekend we went camping?" I actually had no recollection of it. I asked my older girl, Alycia, and she said I was in the tent when they were talking about it.

I even found an email to support the reference to him wanting to go to a Texas Roadhouse. Apparently, Vern was feeling nostalgic for a family vacation he took.

——————

Re: Gilley's Dallas
On Oct 1, 2008, at 11:06 AM, Vern Mascorro wrote:

If we lived in Texas we would be going here. I went here with my parents when I was younger. Urban Cowboy put this place on the map. Does Dan still want to go out on Saturday? It would be fun to take Alycia.
MASCORRO

Explain this to me, bro: how did the medium deliver words from private conversations, because I am desperate to understand this in an earthly kind of way.

How did she get all of the things she got and some not even in my memories? Please, brother, explain this to me, because I can't, and neither can anyone else.

I was clearly overwhelmed with all the unexplained phenomena. My brother was left a little dumbfounded by my reaction and he did not have a clever retort, which we usually enjoy exchanging. Just an "I don't know..."

The depiction from a personality perspective was so accurate. Vickie used some of Vern's actual expressions when speaking in the first person. Vern had a great sense of humor, very clever and sarcastic. He knew how to laugh, have, and poke fun. The many people who knew Vern could attest to this.

He was also a very emotional man. He was deep. And when he was down, he was down. When he was up, he could lift up everyone in the room. Sometimes, he would play super hero with random acts of kindness. He often defended the underdog. He was my hero, in spite of having many human flaws. And best of all, he loved me in spite of all my flaws.

Our relationship was at its peak. We had a twenty-three year courtship, so to speak. When we finally got together it was like magic. We were planning our wedding. Our twenty-three year special bond created the type of comfort and truthfulness that allowed us to be so comfortable and content being our imperfect selves together.

Since we were teenagers, Vern and I shared most every secret, random thought, and introspective observation. The emotions and the words said during the reading referred to this and were completely relevant—it was undeniably him.

He told me on many occasions that I was the only one who truly knew him. He also said it throughout the reading. Vern always felt a pressure to be perfect because so many people looked up to him. He was good at so many things.

The problem with being a super hero is you aren't allowed to be human; it disappoints too many people. He carried that weight and shared it with me. I was always there cheering him on, letting him know it would be okay not to be perfect. I always said, "The higher the pedestal the harder the fall". Vern always felt a little left of center. It took him falling off the pedestal to be comfortable sharing his free spirit with everyone. He had finally reached the time in his life that he was getting comfortable in his skin, and in a flash it was gone. The shock he felt was evident in the reading as he circled around it. It was exactly how I felt as well.

How could anyone know all of this? The answer was truly that only Vern could know, and it was 100% accurate. The message given was pure love but not in a general way. Instead, it was very specific, designed to let me know his consciousness lives on. All that was said was what I needed to hear. It was my lover feeling sad, confused, and angry. He was grieving, just like me. It was the loss of both of our lives.

Whenever I told my incredible connection story, I often got a sympathetic nod. I was tired of people implying that in my grief I was desperate to hear what I wanted to hear. I decided that collecting more proof was necessary. My new mission was to prove something that cannot be proven with circumstantial evidence. I wondered if this reading was a one time anomaly or if there was a whole world full of spirits that I just never had noticed before.

CHAPTER 6: WORLD RELIGIONS—BECOMING A STUDENT

I had no choice but to return to work. However, it was one of those things that did not seem to matter. After my loss, I could not focus, and my co-workers did not know how to relate to or console 'the widow'. I would go to the bathroom during break and cry. I stopped putting my makeup on before work because I would sob on the way to work. In the car I would think about our ride into work together.

I did so enjoy that trip together. We would talk about our plans for the day, and when he dropped me off, he would kiss me and express his love for me. Life does not get any better than that. The fact that this would no longer be, just played through my mind over and over again. Questions of how I could continue without him. I wanted to run away, but I couldn't. I had to support my family. I struggled to get out of bed every morning for three months after he passed. I went through the motions, disassociated.

And then I received a blessing that I did not recognize as one immediately—my work filed Chapter 11, and we all lost our jobs. Though it was the worst possible time to lose my job from a financial standpoint, in hind sight, this cleared the deck, so to speak. It allowed me to focus on things that mattered more. I needed time to heal and feel.

Every night, I closed my eyes and begged God to wake me up from this nightmare. And, if that could not be done, could he at least allow me to escape in my dreams? Maybe I could hear Vern for myself in my dreams. "Oh Lord, please allow me peace in my dreams." I just wanted to sleep and dream of those days and what might have been our future.

I was given the gift of time. I had worked full time since I was 15 years old. When I was young, I was ambitious and in pursuit of material gain. In my current situation, material wealth meant nothing. The challenge was to trust that things would work out and not to fill my thoughts with worry. This was a mistake many of my friends, including my beloved, made when financial disaster befell them. After losing Vern, this latest bad news was very small. I needed to use the time wisely despite my grim financial reality.

During the day, I continued my research on life after death. I think I was looking to reassure myself that Vern would be fine, and I was also looking for a way that I might be able to connect directly with him. I sorted through volumes of information on the religious and cultural views on life after death. I could not get a single theory that completely resonated with me, but the similarities of each religion interested me. The five contemporary religions all made promises of a better state of being after this life, or series of lives, if one modeled their behavior in a certain way.

There are various schools of thought on life after death in the Jewish community. Some Jewish people believe that when we die we go to Olam HaEmet—the World of Truth. When we go, we are given a life review and shown all that we have done in life, good and bad. We are allowed to reflect, and then we are shown the possibilities of the life we would have had if we had we made better choices.

There isn't a hell, per se, but regret for the unrealized potential of the life of better choice. There is actualization of the misdoings in this process. They believe that punishment in a more hell-like state is for only a few really evil souls. For most others, there are levels of heaven. Heaven is felt through your closeness to God's love.

Another group of Jews believe that you are gathered together with your ancestors.

"The dust will return to the ground as it was, and the spirit will return to God who gave it." (Ecclesiastes 12:17)

The Buddhists believe that we reincarnate until we lose desire for earthly things. They believe that desire for earthly things keeps us stuck in the reincarnation cycle. Desire leads to suffering. Life in the body and desire, by its nature, brings suffering. Earthly pleasures are limited in the happiness they can bring. While on earth we suffer a hell-like state with eleven mental and physical afflictions: lust, hatred, illusion, sickness, decay, death, worry, lamentation, pain, melancholy, and grief.

Buddhists do not believe in a soul, as they believe the way to Nirvana is to release the need for a separate identity and to become one with everything and nothing. When one finally releases desire and reaches Enlightenment at the time of death, we return to Source/God/Creator. The ego goes away, and our memory and impulses, which cause our suffering, also go away. Then we can stop reincarnating and stop suffering and go to Nirvana/Heaven. Nirvana is the state of liberation or freedom from desire.

I also read that the Buddhists believe when we pass, we enter into a state of Bardos where we see a clear white light. This phenomenon is described by many religions and by many individuals who have had near death experiences. During Bardos, the spirit does a life review of sorts and returns to earth unless it has ascended to be free from desire. At that time, it can stop reincarnating and move on to paradise, free of the sense of self.

I love the 'live simply and blissfully in the moment' notion and the idea that lust in our hearts for anything is not good. I did not like the end game of Buddhism—it did not seem all that attractive to me. Becoming one with everything and nothing as well as losing all sense of identity, sound like ceasing to exist, or death.

Hindus believe that we reincarnate based on our actions, thoughts, and deeds of our past life. We reincarnate as a result of our 'karma'. A really bad person can reincarnate to a lower form of life such as a mosquito. Hindus believe in a soul they call Atman. Atman is pure and a gift from god. The goal of a Hindu is also to escape the cycle of reincarnation. They believe the cycle of reincarnation, or Samsara, will continue until we understand our true divine nature, which is the pure divine self. Self knowledge is obtained when a person's actions are righteous, serving more than oneself.

When a Hindu dies, he or she is assessed in 4 areas:

Karma yoga: The way of action

Bhakti yoga: The way of devotion

Jnana yoga: The way of knowledge

Raja yoga: The way of meditation

Moksha/Heaven: once the cycle of reincarnation is complete, there are two schools of thought in the Hindu religion. The soul returns to God and either loses its identity and becomes one with God 'Brahman' or retains its identity and lives in an enlightened state with God.

Muslims believe that this life is in preparation for eternal life. Our actions in accordance to holy law will determine our spot in the eternal life. The soul/spirit is the personality, the body is a vessel for the soul. This life is a trial. When one passes, they will eventually face God/Allah. When Allah gathers all of his creations on Judgment Day, The Day of Resurrection, those who have followed God's law and believe in his prophets will gain access to Janna, the Garden of Paradise.

Paradise contains beauty beyond human description. People who were non-believers or evil-doers will not gain access and, instead, go to Jahannam. The time of death is predetermined for everyone. Heaven and Hell have levels of comfort to match your deeds and level of devotion to Islam.

Christians believe that this life is a trial of worthiness, and, at the end, a person's deeds will be judged by God. That person will be given a life review—there are ten commandments used to determine eligibility. A person can break a commandment so long as they repented prior to death and are genuinely sorry for the bad deeds. Some Christians believe in levels, and some believe every person goes to either Heaven or Hell. There are also some Christians who believe that anyone who does not belong to their brand of Christianity will not be eligible to reach the kingdom of heaven, regardless of good deeds.

All of the religions seemed to echo the thought that this life was in preparation for a better life, or state, somewhere else. And that this better life could not be obtained without achieving some state of worthiness in this godforsaken place. For me, it was impossible to imagine a better place than sitting next to my love, experiencing the beauty of earth that I felt on many occasions while we were together. What made it so extra-good was that he made me feel so worthy, just for being me. What could possibly be better than that?

If that was a constant, would we then take it for granted? I wondered if it would feel like heaven. The Buddhists contend that no desire is good desire. I pondered whether desiring a limitless exchange of love was a bad thing. I could see how humans would skew it into a competition, but that is greed not the desire for love.

I also read about the beliefs of afterlife by great human thinkers:

"To sleep, perchance to dream - ay, there's the rub. For in this sleep of death what dreams may come..." - William Shakespeare, Hamlet.

"I regard the brain as a computer which will stop working when its components fail. There is no heaven or afterlife for broken down computers; that is a fairy story for people afraid of the dark." -Stephen Hawking.

"I am ready to meet my Maker. Whether my Maker is prepared for the great ordeal of meeting me is another matter." - Winston Churchill.

"Live as if you were to die tomorrow. Learn as if you were to live forever." -Mahatma Gandhi.

"As a well spent day brings happy sleep, so life well used brings happy death." -Leonardo DaVinci.

"Seeing death as the end of life is like seeing the horizon as the end of the ocean." - David Searls.

"Being a Humanist means trying to behave decently without expectation of rewards or punishment after you are dead." - Kurt Vonnegut.

"The soul takes nothing with her to the next world but her education and her culture. At the beginning of the journey to the next world, one's education and culture can either provide the greatest assistance, or else act as the greatest burden, to the person who has just died." - Plato, The Republic.

"I cannot conceive of a God who rewards and punishes his creatures, or has a will of the kind that we experience in ourselves. Neither can I nor would I want to conceive of an individual that survives his physical death; let feeble souls, from fear or absurd egoism, cherish such thoughts. I am satisfied with the mystery of the eternity of life and with the awareness and a glimpse of the marvelous structure of the existing world, together with the devoted striving to comprehend a portion, be it ever so tiny, of the Reason that manifests itself in nature." – Albert Einstein, The World As I See It.

"I am confident that there truly is such a thing as living again, that the living spring from the dead, and that the souls of the dead are in existence." – Socrates.

I always felt the Existentialist view was just as unlikely as the traditional condemnation models of religion. The assertion that we are random accidents in the universe comes from the same limited knowledge as those of the faithful, but actually makes less sense. Growing up Catholic, I was made to feel any translation of the Bible other than the priest's was false and evil. I always felt that this was powerful mind control for the masses; the idea that listening to anyone but the church doctrine and their interpretation of ancient text made you evil, was absurd to me. I also felt it was absurd that anyone not lucky enough to be born Catholic was going to hell. Despite the fact that I was born and raised into this exclusive club, I chose not to accept this concept and questioned it on many occasions. I would not accept that anyone who was not Catholic was going to hell or at the highest level, Limbo. I recognized that religion is translated through imperfect men with obvious agendas.

The idea of a man in the sky casting down reward and punishment, supporting one class of people or an individual over another, I knew was wrong. It felt wrong; it was not a higher characteristic. This was an act of an insecure being who had to control in order to command respect; a sign of a lowly form. I knew this was not from an exalted being but more a tactic of a power monger trying to gain support through fear and intimidation. I questioned the authority of self-appointed leaders delivering this message from God.

Who among us is worthy to interpret and deliver the word of God to other men? Since all of us are sinners, it's either all of us or none of us.

In today's world, we are actually made to feel stupid for believing in things that cannot be proven within the limits of modern science or experienced through the physical senses. Practically every generation has had theories that have proven to be incorrect as science advances. The only thing that seems stupid to me now is for us to be arrogant enough to think if we cannot explain it—it is false. I love Socrate's quote "The only true wisdom is in knowing you know nothing".

It is important to acknowledge that though there are many things about religions I believe were spun from imperfect, and sometimes downright evil men, there are many higher thinking virtues that are worth basing a life on. I believe our common sense barometer tells us this.

I do feel appreciative of the values I was raised with, which were influenced greatly by Catholicism. I like the symbols of goodness, the meek lamb, the peace dove, and the Mother Mary. Religion, and the sense of community, can be beautiful. It can also give rise to higher thought. Therefore, I believe it can also be a good force in people's lives. I like the fundamental messages like, "Do unto others as you would have them do unto you." If everyone truly practiced this simple truth, we would have heaven here on earth.

Journal Entry: Letter to Vern, Jan 29, 2009

Mascorro my love,

I have been contemplating religion, philosophy, and why we are here, all discussions we have had before. I always loved your inner knowing, your wisdom, your ability to trust and seek within. You had a knowledge of the grander scheme that seemed to come from nowhere, no doctrine, no teacher. You would say such wise things, and you would trust even when you could find no reasonable explanation. You would say the creator would not let us experience this pain if it were not for our benefit. Is it true, baby? I wish I could hear your answer.

I just want you to know I will always appreciate your optimism, I know everything is about perspective because this is at the core of whether we will allow ourselves to experience joy.

Despite all the adversity you had experienced, you rose out of ashes still an optimist. You are truly a phoenix. Your knowing and faith that we could rise above anything was one of your biggest gifts to me. You always believed that good things would come out of bad, that knowledge could be gained through firsthand experience and that knowledge would only make us better people.

I got laid off. I can hear you saying, "Don't worry, lover, it will all work out." I will trust it will all work out, as you always encouraged me to believe that it will.

I miss you so,
Love, Darcy

———————

From: Vern Mascorro
Date: Oct 27, 2008 11:44 AM PDT
To: Darcy Bellows
Subject: All is well. I assure you.

Lover, all will work out well. I will pick you up when you call and we will be off for a dollar meal lunch (HAHAHA).

Never worry, but allow your concern to move us in a positive and correct direction. Again lover, all will work out. You and I both have been in uglier situations. We for sure will land on our feet with putting our heads together and working on the same page.

Love YA!
MASCORRO

———————

I clung to the email Vern sent only three days prior to his leaving this earth.

I learned from Vern that we could get through anything and that the world can be a vast frontier if we see it that way. He made me believe that we are capable of moving beyond our losses and failures if we choose.

How would I do it without my greatest support? He made me feel special, like I was beautiful and capable of anything.

If I could share a secret to our everlasting love, it was our genuine appreciation and support for one another. I could hear him urging me forward.

CHAPTER 7: THE AIRY-FAIRY STUFF

Journal Entry: Letter to Vern, February 3, 2009

My Love,

I've been spending my time reading about how to hear you on the other side like the mediums. The theory is that we all have a sixth sense. I can recall many stories when our individual instincts had proven invaluable. We both caught ex-lovers in lies through pure psychic intuition.

According to what I've read, intuition is our sixth sense, and the same sense that is used to communicate with spirits. The secret to hearing you is to learn to clear the mind enough to not have conscious thoughts running through it, meditate. Meditation is the art of clearing your mind and my mind never seems to stop. I have conjured up the courage to join a couple of groups that might assist in my ability to receive messages from you.

I must admit, I had preconceived notions of the type of people that might attend these groups. I'm picturing old hippies dropping LSD, becoming one with the god that visited them in the form of a giant Raggedy Ann doll. Or maybe a group of airy fairy new-agers with a blank look on their faces, as if they had just returned from having a mind meld on the mother ship from the planet Zarton. Or maybe a group of Goths fascinated with vampires and witchcraft.

I imagine you asking me if just fell off the turnip truck with all these stereotypes. You were so good at challenging stupid assumptions. You helped me grow so much. The small world I grew up in suddenly became so large once you graced my life. Oh so grateful, I hope I made you feel that when you were alive.

I love you eternally,
Bellows

____

The first group I joined, the people graciously opened their homes to anyone wanting to learn about meditation. They were not selling anything and were not benefiting in anyway. In my jaded thoughts, I was wondering what their angle was. I thought, "Are they swingers trying to get us relaxed and loose? Or were they going steal our money while we were clearing our minds? Were they going to play subliminal messages that would have us join some cult religion?" My cynical thoughts couldn't have been further from the truth. I found people who had benefited from the practice of meditation. They told me that the benefits included stress reduction and a feeling of peace and ease. I knew I could use a feeling of peace and ease right about then. I asked if it helped in communicating with spirits, and they said that many have reported spiritual experiences.

We were instructed to relax and let all thought go, to release all worldly and material concerns and just to be. Focus on the breath, breathe in and out until all thought disappeared and your worry fell away.

Well, my busy, logical mind could not have had a less successful first attempt at trying to meditate. I sat in the lotus position trying to blank out my mind, but my mind began to wonder all over the place. One minute I was thinking of the fact that I needed to exercise. I tried to blank it out by silently saying aums in my head but then I laughed at myself for being silly. I wondered if everyone could hear my gulping and breathing as loudly as I was hearing it. It was beginning to annoy me. Then my back started hurting, so I began shifting to get comfortable. I actually felt a little anxiety with my failure to relax and meditate; the exact opposite of the peace you were supposed to get.

Meditation was not going to be easy for me, but my determined nature would not let me stop at my first failed attempt. In the books I read, they equated learning to meditate to learning how to play the piano. Anyone can learn to play if they practice. They might not be Mozart, but they can certainly learn to play a few tunes.

Journal Entry: Letter to Vern, February 10, 2009

My Love,

My fears about what type of people I would encounter in my new meditation efforts were laid to rest; I found people searching for answers just like myself. I found I had more in common with some of these folks than co-workers or certain family members. There is a bond when you meet others asking bigger questions in life like, "Why are we here?" and "What does it mean?"

I found sincerity, open minds and open hearts, which is very disarming. Although I did not get the peaceful benefits of meditation, I did meet some great people and I ended up speaking to a woman after class. She was there for the same reason I came for. She had lost her daughter at an unnatural time and was in search of answers about life and its meaning. Her daughter had passed a couple of years ago and she was set on finding her as well. I told her about my reading with Vickie to give her hope. I know we can help each other. I told her I was interested in starting a development circle but I wasn't sure where to start. She said she would be very interested if I found the right group of positive people.

I told her I had joined a paranormal research group so I can meet some people that may know where to find a development circle. She said the ghost and witch stuff scared her, so she wasn't interested in that. I told her I wasn't either but that the research is related and I was sure that my man would be by my side protecting me and helping me discern.

Yours eternally,
Bellows

No sooner did I write about the challenge of finding a psychic development circle and boom, a week later I received a message from a woman in the paranormal group I joined. I soon found out that this kind of synchronicity, the "ask and it is given" mentality is what the new-agers term "being in the flow". My flow came with ease once I took an interest. It was really that simple.

Feb 11, 2009: Meet up Message

Hi Darcy,

I am a member of the Paranormal Messengers group. I am starting a psychic development circle. Is this something you might be interested in? I have been a practicing medium for about 7 years and I feel ready to start sharing what I've learned. Let me know if this is something you might be interested in.

Blessings,
Michelle

Hi Michelle,

Well, talk about synchronicity. I recently joined this paranormal research group for the sole purpose of finding some people to start a psychic development circle with. Count me in! Let me know how I can help get it started. I am open to hosting at my house.

Kind Regards,
Darcy

Feb 15, 2009

Hi Darcy,

I think this is really going to be an awesome psychic circle, and I am looking forward to us all growing together! As of right now, I think I have four people interested. I was looking at the calendar and March 7th, the first Sat. in March looks good for our first meeting. Does that work for you? Maybe by then I will have more people as well. I think we should go ahead and meet to get started. We can meet at my house once a month as well. I live in Lemoore, so not too far. I am thinking 10 people should be the limit for now.

Okay, now this might sound crazy, but I have to ask. I also do spirit/psychic sketch art. This all started for me this last December. My guides have been trying to get me to do this for three years now, but I just would not listen. I never thought I could draw anything but stars and heart doodles. lol. I now draw portraits of people that I see in my mind's eye. If I see someone, I draw them and I don't always know who they are or who they go with. I have done this and found out later who they were. I am still learning how this is all works for me. lol. If someone needs a reading, sometimes they will show up and want to be drawn for that particular person then I know who they are. Then I draw them usually the week before the reading and then take the sketch to the reading to get validation. It is a huge validation!

Well the reason I am telling you this is because I was supposed to do a reading today, but it got cancelled. Well, this morning, right before I woke up, I saw this man really clear in my mind's eye. This man seemed to direct me to you because right after that, I woke up and your name entered my mind.

When I saw him he showed me himself from side profile view and I always sketch from a front facial view so my sketch might be off a little bit. All I know is he has black hair, parted on the side and his jaw line is strong and I really noticed his crow's feet lines, maybe he was smiling big. His skin seemed to be tan as well. I got up and sketched him in hopes on finding out who he goes with. I thought I would ask you if you want to see him to see if maybe he is for you? I can email the sketch to you. I try to get as close as I can but sometimes my sketches just resemble the person because I am drawing from my mind with nothing in front of me to look at. I try to get the shape of the face, eyes, hair and mouth as close as I can. I have done a few that were right on, so who knows? While sketching, I also heard the name Jim, does that mean anything to you?

Thanks Darcy!

Blessing,
Michelle

____

Sun, Feb 15, 2009, 10:34 PM

From: Darcy Bellows <darcybellows@mac.com>

Subject: available to assist

Michelle,

I just got laid off from work, so I am available to assist in organization and hosting of the development circle.

I am dumbfounded. The description of the man that came to you and left you my name, this is a match to my fiancé who was just killed in a car accident a little over three months ago. I was looking at a side profile of his picture on my desk as I was reading the email. In the picture, he is smiling, so you can see his beautiful crow's feet by his eyes. He has black hair and tan skin and a very strong jaw line. I got chills up and down the side of my head as I was reading your email.

Thank you for finding me and giving me this message. It's hard to believe. It seems like Vern deliberately put us together. As I mentioned last week, when you first contacted me, the only reason I joined the paranormal research group was to find people interested in starting a development group. It looks like I am getting a little help. This is too amazing and coincidental.

I can't wait to meet you. Thank you again!

Kind Regards,
Darcy

Immediately following this miracle introduction, I went online and I looked up 'spirit channeling'. I wanted to understand how Michelle was able to see spirits well enough to draw them. The first Google result was a book called Tale of Two Brothers by Jacqueline Murray. I read the summary of the book and, remarkably, it was a channeling from Jim Morrison, one of my all-time favorite famous people. In fact, I wrote my senior paper in high school on Jim Morrison's legacy.

In my paper, I focused on the social changes in society that he helped influence through his art. I took the focus off his rock-star image and instead placed it on what I believe was his gift. Jim helped evoke intellectual curiosity in me. I read books that I would never have read had I not been interested in Jim Morrison's work and how his music and poetry came to be. Through his influence I read authors like

Jack Kerouac, Aldous Huxley, and Franz Kafka. I read poets like William Blake and Arthur Rimbaud and philosophers like Friedrich Nietzsche and Jean-Paul Sartre. Jim Morrison was a major influence on my young mind that grew up in a very homogenous blue collar suburb of Minneapolis. Although I thought some of what I read was weird, it cultivated the artist inside me and helped give way to the freedom of expression I possess today.

It suddenly occurred to me that Michelle had just written me asking me about a Jim. She said, "While sketching, I also heard the name Jim, does that mean anything to you?" I got the chills. Obviously, I was interested in the content, but it was a coincidence I couldn't ignore, so I clicked the link to look at the preview. I read that the author was a reluctant channel for Jim Morrison. The author said she was never a fan of his music and had little knowledge of his history, which was good because she couldn't be a good channel if she was front loaded with pre-conceived notions. She said that the book was channeled because Jim wanted to set the record straight about his life, death, and legacy. He said no one really knew him because of the charismatic front he was always putting on. This was very similar to Vern's feelings on the matter. I wondered how many other magnanimous personalities throughout history felt this sort of loneliness.

In this book, Jim Morrison tells his story through the channel from his now spiritual perspective. He also takes the opportunity to tell the reader about the afterlife and what philosophical theories to read for better understanding, which I found fascinating. The book had a surprising twist. He was channeling for the expected reasons stated above, but the most important motive for his channeling was to get communication to his twin flame who he had been separated from because of his early demise. He wrote letters to her much like I was doing with Vern. I was so completely immersed in the preview that I barely surfaced for two days; I did not realize that this preview was 437 pages long. The story was so relevant to me, it was almost too coincidental.

I told my new friend Michelle about the book and she asked, "Do you think that is the 'Jim' Vern was talking about while sketching?"

"I don't know," I said, "but I ordered the book. You should check out the preview, it's really good." It had a lot of interesting theories about the purpose of life and what happens in the afterlife. I went to send her the link and I could now only see twenty pages before I got a dialog box prompting me to buy the book if I wanted to read more. I anonymously signed on from another computer, and I got the same dialog box after clicking on about 20 pages again. I don't know if getting the whole book was a technical glitch or a present from beyond, but the magic of being at the right place at the right time did not elude me.

Journal Entry: Letter to Vern, February 16, 2009

Mascorro my love,

I met Michelle, the lady you appear to have sent to help me, for coffee. We were instant friends, almost like long lost sisters picking up where we left off. She is a very genuine person; someone I can see us getting on well with. Evidently, she lost her brother, Mike, in a car accident. The night he died, she sensed it and shortly after was given a vivid vision of the accident scene. Michelle said she was always intuitive and was attracted to angels and other positive mystical things, but she never really put much energy into learning about it until her brother Mike died. This loss was the catalyst that put Michelle on her journey for answers on life and death, much like mine. She has since done some amazing things. She has learned how to connect to spirits and does spirit art, which means she can draw who she sees in spirit. At our first meeting, she showed me drawings she had done for a few of her clients' deceased loved ones, and they were very good matches to the pictures provided after the fact.

She asked if you wore cologne that was in a square bottle in a nice square packaging. I told her yes that was the cologne I had purchased for you and that you had saved every bottle and box. It reminded me how much you loved smart packaging and marketing. Every time you would see a service or product, your mind would be spinning. You would always know how to make it better or give credit when credit was due. I felt sad for all the great business ideas and conversations we would not have, yet appreciative for the ones we did. I don't know if I told you how much I admired your business savvy. I hope you could see it in my eyes as I watched you in action, or as we discussed your latest idea or critique of a new business. I watched you adoringly many nights as you shared great insights of all kinds. I welled with pride as if I had something to do with it.

I enjoyed your enthusiasm, your passion for everything you did; it was contagious. I have lost my appetite without you.

I have allowed myself to start believing that miracles, things I cannot see or understand, are possible. I absolutely loved the book Tale of Two Brothers, if that is what you intended to send me. It was well received and understood.

Yours Eternally,
Darcy

On the day of our first circle, upon arriving, Michelle gave me some very specific information about Vern. She asked, "Did Vern use to cut the sleeves off his t-shirts?"

I said, "Yes, I have closets full of cut-off t-shirts."

Michelle said, "Yeah, I saw him take a t-shirt and cut off the sleeves and then wear it on the way over. He says it made him feel manly like the muscle shirts."

"I know, I thought so, too," I said, and giggled at the thought. I knew Vern would be with us today as we started our new adventure.

We had only four additional people come. We opened our circle with a prayer of protection and a request for guidance from the Highers, coming from peace and light. We gave everyone a moment to request assistance and strength from their own deity. I remember as a child calling to Jesus, Mary, and the angels for protection from the monsters in my nightmares. I remember it was quite effective in turning the nightmare around, so why not try it here.

Michelle brought a guided meditation that instructed us to ground ourselves to the earth and get into a state of 'higher vibration' and to be open. I sat in prayer since I could not concentrate on the guided meditation and blank out at the same time. We proceeded to do an exercise called psychometry. You take a piece of jewelry or something worn, held, or meaningful from the sitter (a receiver of a reading). The idea is that our objects hold energy. Each person in the circle put a personal object into the bowl and we passed it around and took one out that was not ours.

When I got my object, I felt nothing different when I touched it. Inside my head I thought "OK, Vern. Help me, baby". A string of words that didn't make much sense to me flowed and then stopped after a little over a dozen. They were not necessarily related words. I didn't feel like I got anything. It felt like I made up random words but I recorded them anyway as instructed by Michelle.

Light turns on-Ideas

Clever

Stillness

Ride

Hope

Anger need to relax

Sequoia

Silver Hair

Gentle Persuasion

Grass

Knight in Shining Armor

Sitting still contemplate

Tulips

Ronnie, white male heavy-set

The song "Mustang Sally" came in my head

These seemingly random words made the sitter very emotional. She found homes for each one. She spoke through them revealing a piece of her heart. The emotion in the room was very heavy.

The word Ideas: she was in a period of transition, thinking about new business ideas, hence idea and being clever. She found her best ideas and healing in stillness and contemplation and had been doing so plenty lately. She often sat outside, surrounded by grass and tulips in her yard. None of this would have been impressive to me so far but the last two phrases were shockers, plus the 'Knight in shining armor' phrase. This lady shared that early in her life she had lost the love of her life and her brother all in one night. Her brother had a classic Mustang. He and her fiancé had gone for a ride not to return, they were killed in a car crash.

I sat stunned. I felt no emotion connected to these phrases, but I sure felt it as she told her story. I cried along with the four other women in the room. This was a cathartic experience for each of us. A skeptic may not have been impressed with my reading, but I sure was. More importantly, it connected to this woman who had a tragedy befall her life so many years ago, and now she would get a chance to heal, to heal with strangers. This was a miracle in and of itself.

Journal Entry: Letter to Vern, February 27, 2009

Mascorro My Love,

I found genuine real people willing to hope in spite of disappointment and tragedy, wanting to heal and be healed. The spirit circle was profound. I wish I could have shared this experience with you beside me. You were the first I would run to with any new experiences, far or near. We would share new experiences together. We had so many firsts along the way. I do understand you are beside me, but I am still a simple creature. If I cannot see it, I do not experience it.

If spirit communication is just a bunch of thoughts landing in your head, I will never be able to tell if you are speaking to me, because there is never a moment you are not in my conscious thoughts. I always imagine what you would say in almost every situation. I always have since the minute I laid eyes on you.

I wasn't thinking I got much, but I actually got a name of the brother that passed. I really did not see or hear anything, all I can say is it felt like I was making stuff up. I need a more visceral experience to believe it. I need 3D visions or something spectacular to tell me it's coming from you. I need the experience to make me feel like your touch made me feel.

Yours Eternally, Bellows

I did Psychic Circle every other week for the rest of my stay in Fresno through August. This helped provide relief from the hell I was going through packing up Vern's and my life. I learned a lot about the process of connecting to spirits. It really came down to suspending belief that you can receive messages and then putting yourself in a state of stillness. And then practice. You have to shut off all your external perceptions and just write down what comes to mind. I didn't get overpowering feelings or anything to suggest that what I was getting belonged to anyone, but almost every time, it did. Whenever we would have a new person start they would always say, "I didn't get anything," but they almost always did.

Every meeting was incredibly healing for everyone involved. On the second or third meeting, Michelle brought a sketch for one of the ladies who had lost her daughter.

Michelle had received a dream vision to draw a woman and was told it was for a lady from circle. Michelle assumed the drawing was of the lady's daughter. So Michelle showed the drawing to our new friend, and she did not recognize it to be her daughter. So we were stumped. Thus far, Michelle had a pretty high accuracy in making connections with the drawings. We asked to see family pictures, and lo and behold, she pulled out a picture of her granddaughter—her deceased daughter's child. Bingo! Everyone in the room except the sitter saw it without a doubt. Michelle had captured the essence of the granddaughter. It was not photo perfect, but all the main features were captured, down to the hairstyle. Michelle was surprised because she had not experienced spirits showing anyone but themselves.

Sketching a spirit from a vision that flashes in the third eye is an incredible feat, and what a gift of proof for someone to receive. Everyone but the sitter saw the incredible resemblance of the sketch to her granddaughter. I don't know if it was because it wasn't photo-realistic, but the features were illustrated very well in their basic form. Our friend was particularly skeptical. She had grown up in a strict religious faith that gave no power to the individual to talk or feel God without a middle man to interpret. Only men that proclaimed themselves appointed were allowed to speak to God directly.

I noticed an increase in accuracy and specific information, not only for myself, but the entire group. I noticed everyone had their own style and perceptions. I developed a routine: I asked three things of Vern in my mind. I would say, "Okay, baby, first give me something so they know I am connected. Give me as much as possible and make it specific. Show me a situation I could not know about." Then I would ask, "What do they need to know?" I would often get a song.

I remember getting the song "You've lost that loving feeling...bring back that loving feeling, before it's gone, gone, gone," for a woman and she said, "I am not in a relationship. I don't know what it means." One of her good friends was with her in the room and she successfully interpreted the song. She said, "It's been nine years since she has even looked at a man. Her life is all about her kids, and her kids are grown up. It's time she builds a life for herself and she needs to bring back that loving feeling. It's about time, don't you think?"

Between development sessions, I tried myself to communicate with Vern. I tried automatic writing. Michelle taught me to get into a relaxed state and meditate for 5-10 minutes. She said to ask guides or loved ones to write with you and let them take over the pen.

I tried this, but nothing automatically flowed. Michelle suggested doodling until either thoughts flow or you feel the pen go. So I did this, I got beautiful words in my mind that I know Vern would say. But that's just it; these were statements I knew he would say. It was clear it was very difficult to separate your invested conscious thoughts from this very subtle practice of spirit communication.

When I was not associated at all with the person, it was a lot easier to let it flow without your mind entering in or filling in the gaps of the story. I gave myself a test. "Tell me something that is going to happen in the next couple days." I felt that Alycia (my older daughter) would call with good news. No call, test failed.

Ugh! No dreams, no direct communication. I have heard that those in heavy grief cannot get there. The theory is that those of us in heavy grief cannot vibrate high enough to get to the other side. Although I believed I discredited this account by making several strong connections for people not associated with me.

My observation was that it was almost impossible to read for myself. I would fill in gaps with my conscious desires. The fact is, I was invested with myself. It was too hard to remain impartial or neutral; I would only hear what was already in my head, and there in lies the art of being a medium. I was, however, too stubborn to stop trying.

CHAPTER 8: DISCERNMENT

In my research efforts, I ended up receiving readings from forty-five different readers. Only five made a connection. A few more got a few general facts correct, but just as many incorrect. Twenty-two got nothing I could recognize as Vern. Finding a medium who has the ability to be a medium without putting themselves in the middle, is very difficult. It is refined art to be sure.

I have learned we all have the ability to connect, but it is truly a gift, or a practiced art, to be able to remove oneself and let the messages flow without getting personal beliefs or interpretations in the middle.

People who are grieving, including myself, want the connection so badly we will give too much information. There are so many people out there claiming to have this ability—and they probably do from time to time, but sometimes we can't help but be human and let our egos and beliefs get wrapped up in the reading. This can even happen to well-practiced and connected mediums, which is why they, too, can occasionally get a couple of things wrong or have an off reading or day. It's just like any other gift or skill.

Beware of Phishing: Phishing is the process where the Reader asks questions until they can deduce what you came for or what you want to hear.

I have had some of the mediums start the reading with a disclaimer: "The person you are looking for may or may not come because they have free will." In truth, the reader may or may not get a connection. If they are connected at the moment of your reading, your loved one will come. If a reader starts the reading with this, it is a concern for me. It points to the reader being in the ego. In my experience, the ones who were able to connect to Vern got Vern very strongly. The evidence was specific and clear.

The unconnected medium may reference extended family that the sitter really doesn't have a clue about. A bad reading might go something like this.

UM: "I see a father figure. A quiet type, has your father passed?"

S: "No."

UM: "Hmmm. Yeah, maybe it's a close uncle or someone who acted like a father figure. I am getting a J name, John or James." (These are two very common names from this century).

S: "I don't know who you are talking about."

UM: "Did your Dad have any friends that have passed with that name?"

S: "No, I have a great uncle Joe that passed."

UM: "Oh that's it! Tell your father his uncle says hello."

Beware of Grief Counseling 101. The reader may give you standard advice from 'spirits' based on the principles of grief counseling. The message will be based on an effort to get you to move forward and they will make general statements like, "Your loved one wants you to know there was no pain, it was painless. He is doing fine. He is always with you and loves you. He wants you to know he expects you to love again. He has other things to do, so you must let go." This information is way too general even if it has a shred of truth. If they haven't provided specific details about that person you are seeking, there simply is no evidence they are connected to your loved one.

They may also state other general facts like, "He died from something in the chest or lungs." Heart and respiratory failure is part of the death process. We may want to focus on other bits of evidence, the specifics of the passing, sudden accident or an unexpected injury. The medium Vickie not only identified that Vern got in an accident but even got the specifics of the accident. Sometimes, a specific disease is difficult for a non-medical professional to name exactly, so close does count in this case.

Don't let the reader get away with general personality traits. If they start and are too general, say, "Tell me more. Tell me something more specific." They may give general desirable personality traits that anyone wanting connection to their loved one would attribute to them, like: "He was kind and loving; he cared about his family deeply." This, in my mind, is something anyone would believe about their beloved. Lead the reader to more specifics by saying, "Yes, can you get more specific?"

I also notice that even if you have a great medium with a good connection, there can be misses from both the reader and the sitter. Sometimes as a sitter (a receiver of a reading), you are given incredible evidence, and it eludes you because you were looking for something else. Put your expectations aside and listen. If something doesn't make sense, don't dismiss it right away. Ask for more information. If it still doesn't make sense, put it aside, listen again, and sometimes it will come up. Occasionally even great mediums will get their own mind entangled in a reading. They may add a word or misinterpret a vision slightly, so close counts if they established credibility with many hits.

I absolutely encourage everyone to be open to receiving an experience with their loved ones from the other side. In fact, I know with certainty that if you look, are open, and are in need, you will find it. I had a friend ask me one time, "Aren't you avoiding closure?" I thought for a moment and replied, "No, I don't seek closure. That is a clinical term used by health professionals not invested in anything." I shook my head and scoffed, "Closure, I am glad that you do not understand the absurd nature of your inquiry. Do I understand that my lover is physically dead and that this is a part of the process here on earth? Yep I do."

Journal Entry: Letter to Vern, March 4, 2009

Lover,

So many people do not understand why I would want to remain connected after your physical body was laid to rest. You were not the sum total of your body. If they loved their mate like I love you, I know they would understand. I had too many years tucking my feelings away for you, so much wasted time. I finally collect the courage to put my heart on the line, and I experienced the happiest time of life. Then, in a flash it was gone. People try to make sense of it; I still cannot. Every reading, I get clear evidence you seem to be equally mystified by our sudden reversal of fortune. I try to remember and hear your wisdom, your peace in knowing everything happens for a reason. My love, I have yet to be convinced.

Eternally yours,
Bellows

CHAPTER 9: NEW QUESTIONS

When someone close dies, you often think about the what-ifs and wonder was he satisfied with this life, did he have any regrets? Is he happy where he is now? Where is he, floating on a cloud? Does he feel a little lost like me? If he had regrets, did he want to talk through them like he did in life? I really wanted to understand what Vern was going through. Was he still adjusting as I was? I actually wrote these questions down and tried to get answers for myself, but my mind drew blank. So I got another reading.

My next reading with Vickie Gay almost magically brought light to the questions I had written down. I did not speak of what I wanted to know, nor did I identify myself as a repeat customer. This was my third reading so I am not sure if she knew who I was. It had been two months since the second reading, and Vickie did readings daily.

As she started the reading, she saw a younger gentlemen holding my head up. That image made her cry.

She said she saw him touching my jaw, she said there is a zit on the right side bothering you. She said this is to show you he is near you. Vickie had not been in the room and had no way of knowing that two minutes prior to the reading, I was in the bathroom picking a zit on the right side of my jaw. She then said, "The love is too strong for the separation." She channeled "'I am upset and angry with myself because I am over here'."

I assured him that it was an accident. He said he knew that, he was just upset that he did not grow old. He said, through Vickie, "'If I had known, I would have gone faster, gotten to the point faster'." I believe he was referring to our union and the fact that we were just going to be married and were planning on having a child.

"'I would have done things differently. The life would be with you, but much sooner, more focused on what matters'." I cried so hard—this was the same regret I felt deep in my heart and everything I wanted to hear.

Some of the rest of the reading was centered on methods I could employ to hear him for myself. He explained that when I focused thought on him, he could feel me. He said that I should be able to sense him as well if I learned how to blank out and be in bliss with him.

She described his animated personality, he was talking with his hands and saying that he was as sharp as he ever was, "'I'll figure this out so we can make a connection'." I actually had heard Vern say the phrase "I am feeling as sharp as ever" in reference to himself a few months prior to the accident.

VG: "He is sorry that he left you. He is okay. He is not okay with the fact that he had to leave you here in the physical. He said you are grieving so hard that you cannot see opportunities. He misses your tender touch and your soft hands. There are a lot of little things he's remembering now that he took for granted would always be there."

D: "Me too."

VG: "He still does not have satisfaction in the expression of his life and his love for you. He knew he got better. He just wants to express his love for you."

D: "I love him too."

VG: "Ahh, he just licked you…I don't know what that was all about."

D: (I laugh) "I actually have a picture of that."

VG: "I see eyebrows that look like moustaches, very thick heavy eyebrows."

D: "Yes. He had thick heavy eyebrows."

VG: "Yes, that look like a moustache?"

D: "I don't think they did."

VG: "He said, 'They're my eyebrows'."

(This is the part where Michelle and Vickie match in readings done a week apart.)

D: "How does he get along? I can't seem to get through the day."

VG: "He feels your sorrow. Even though he is alive, he is not in the physical, and you miss that. He is sorry."

D: "We are parted. I am not able to hear him. He was my life."

I received many readings from Vickie. She almost always brought some piece of evidence that blew my mind, but her most precious gift was her uncanny ability to channel him. At times she seemed to be talking for him with his words. She picked up his emotions and allowed him to flow through her.

Journal Entry: Letter to Vern, March 27, 2009

Mascorro,
I am so sorry this happened to us too. We had so much left to do and say. We were both getting better at expressing ourselves. We were both getting better at working as a team. We were both discovering the joy of giving.

I didn't tell you often enough how amazing I thought you were, I just assumed someone as magical as you would know it. That assumption is flawed. We all like to hear it, no matter how fabulous we are. The year before you died, you said to me that you wished you saw yourself the way I saw you, and then today in the reading you told me that again.

Vern Albert Mascorro, you were, and are, truly an amazing human being. You will always be my hero in your splendid imperfection. You were everything I aspired to be, minus a few things :). I miss inspiration being part of the Mascorro "royal" court. The world around me could be ordinary and mundane, but the minute I sat in your presence, I was transformed.

I relate to the lyrics in "Going to California," by Led Zeppelin, as the lonely queen had no king, melancholy filled her days. Darling, I know time is a friend in this case as you get used to what is, we just had so much left to do.

Yours Eternally, Darcy

Though the why of my misfortune was not clear, my new mission was. I must learn more and share. I was so lucky to meet a group of people as willing and open to explore as I was. Some would say it was not luck at all; that it was all serendipitous. I knew my new openness to the miracles life can bring forth played into my new found luck or awareness, whatever your perspective.

Michelle did this work from her heart. She wanted to ensure anyone who needed a connection, got it. She was focused on helping as many people as possible.

We talked about how awesome it would be to have a center for the bereaved to visit. I would hear people say, "If this is a gift from God, it should be offered free." Yet a church, a preacher, a healer, or a doctor of any kind has to get paid for their service in order to survive. A preacher gets donations; a doctor charges a healthy fee to pay back his education. This gift is no different, it's just a delicate time and a delicate matter, and it is hard to ask for money. Michelle worked full-time and did the readings on the side so she could keep them affordable but that left only a few hours a week for such an important service. Her passion was making connections. She just couldn't afford to do it full-time.

Michelle and I started to envision a foundation, a non-profit, that one day could be the healing center people could go to. Michelle and I started small, which is the only way to start when you have a good idea. For now I was feeling fortunate to have met a woman like her. What if everyone had the fortune of having access to people like this? It would make life and death transformations so much less traumatic.

I still couldn't believe the circumstance of our meeting. Michelle was as open to exploration as I was when she read for me. She placed no preconceived notions on what should be said. She, too, was an explorer. She wasn't wrapped in her beliefs or about being right, she was truly open.

My two favorite mediums, Michelle and Vickie, had styles that were different. But both seemed to achieve a connection and get specific details that were relevant to Vern and me. Michelle was self-taught. She had spent several years studying after she had a precognitive vision of her brother's accident, and then visits after that. In my research, the quality of the connection was not determined by price or notoriety of the medium. One might ask who to pick? Use your gut reaction or referral. Listening to your intution is more difficult than one would think because sometimes we want something so badly the noise in our mind makes it impossible to hear our spirit.

Michelle's readings always provided evidence. She would get a series of visual impressions in her head or would hear words or feel the feelings of the spirit. Vickie also got images, words and feelings directed from the spirit. In addition, she would go in and out of a semi-trance and actually channel the spirit's words as if she were the spirit. The spirit's emotions would overtake her. Both gifts were amazing. The delivery was different, but the content seemed directed by Vern.

It is clear that a reading is impacted by the reader's frame of reference and personality.

Michelle prepared for a reading with a 10-15 minute meditation and did an automatic writing session prior to the call. So she was usually ready with some items. It helped her feel at ease and less on-the-spot. It flowed automatically once she got going.

M: "What's this about the dog? The dog is running up like it has way too much energy."

D: "Yes, I am fixing stuff the dog broke this week. It's only a year and a half old. My friend Blake replaced the sprinkler heads and the screens. A polite way to put it is to say, 'She had too much energy'."

M: "Did you have to bury holes?"

D: "Yes, Blake did that."

M: "He said something about planting flowers. Not roses, but daisies."

D: "Yes, we planted the daisies in the backyard, but they haven't bloomed yet. Daisies were Vern's favorite flowers."

M: "He is showing me a billfold, wallet, or something. It has a lot of stuff in it."

D: "I think it's his organizer, it's wallet-sized. When you said that, the organizer paper moved. His wallet is on top of his organizer and both are sitting right in front of me."

M: "Wow, now he is showing a white envelope."

D: "There is a white bag with his hair in it also in front of me."

M: "I feel like you will find something in an envelope later. It feels important. And now you are eating an ice cream cone."

D: "Oh my, while you were talking I was looking through his wallet, and I just found a free Baskin Robbins coupon in a white envelope, almost at the same time you mentioned the ice cream cone.

M: "Now I'm seeing scissors. It's like he's showing paper cut outs, like someone cut a design out of paper."

D: "Again, wow! Right here on the desk there are two paper snowflakes Gabby cut out and brought to me."

M: (She laughs excitedly.) "That's basically what he is showing me, a folded paper that you cut pieces out of and open it up to a design."

D: "That's exactly right, it's right here."

M: "Wow, he is good!"

D: "So he is basically showing you everything that is around me, proving he is here?"

M: "Yep."

D: "Oh, there is CD in a white envelope. It is an archive of photos of him."

M: "What about watercolor pens, thicker watercolor pens that you would color a picture with?"

D: "I have those supplies, but in front of me is a spiritual book with artwork that looks like it could have been created with those pens. Gabby pointed to it as you were saying it. That, too, is on the desk where he seems to be pointing things out."

M: "Oh that makes sense. He is showing me an all color picture.

Egghead or eggshell...did anyone ever decorate an egg with a face on it?"

D: "Yes, I have it in a picture."

M: "Do you have a bible or a large book nearby?"

D: "I have a 700-page book on my nightstand. The Tale of Two Brothers, I told you about."

M: "Are you painting?"

D: "Yes, I just did one, and I recently hung it."

M: "I feel like he wants you to do that to take your mind off things.

Now I see a suitcase."

D: "We are moving."

M: "What's the joke about the Groucho Marx's eyebrows? Thick, black eyebrows."

D: "It's him, he showed those to Vickie (the other medium), too, during the last reading."

M: "He is moving the eyebrows up and down."

D: "He showed Vickie that too!

He was very expressive with his eyebrows. He used to give the Spock look which I couldn't do. Vickie thought it was a moustache but then corrected herself in her last reading."

M: "He is laughing about it."

D: "He had great eyebrows."

M: "What about Snoopy? And the Red Baron?"

D: "Can't think of anything right now."

M: "I drew Snoopy, and I heard the Red Baron. So something will pop up."

Though I could not place this while she was reading, his parents had gone to Knott's Berry Farm and called to tell me about it a couple weeks later. The Peanuts characters are featured there.

M: "Did he ride a bicycle?"

D: "Yes he did. That and running were his main exercises, he did them every day. A guy asked yesterday if he could have the bicycles. He was a worker, so I gave them to him."

M: "Oh! He used to run the dog with the bike. So she wouldn't tear up the yard."

D: "Exactly. Yes, he did that to wear her out."

M: "Was he going to make a kennel?"

D: "Yes, tell him that is where she's staying now, his stepdad built a new one for her."

M: "What's the deal with the Playboy bunny?"

D: "Alycia has the logo hanging in her room. She likes the show The Girls Next Door."

M: "Is there a collar around it with studs?"

D: "Yes, Vern and Alycia bought Princess a studded collar. The dog has outgrown it so Alycia has it hanging in her room."

M: "I'm seeing a coffee can with a lid on it."

D: "There is a Christmas tin that his mom gave us with a lid."

M: "I don't know."

M: "Did he have a knife with sentimental value like a pocketknife?"

D: "Yes."

M: "Like it's passed down."

It has an abalone cover on it. It's something important, like an heirloom that was passed down. Like someone in the family gave it to him."

D: "Yes!"

M: "I am seeing a coin collection. Are they in plastic sheeting?"

D: "My aunt that has passed gave me those."

M: "You're not going to believe this, but now I am seeing toilet paper."

D: (I chuckle) "Even more strange, I know what that is. He would not use toilet paper. He said it felt like sandpaper, so he would tell all guests that visited our house that they needed to experience the new disposable wipes in lieu of toilet paper. He would bring out the box and tell everyone that came over that the wipes would change their life. He was hilarious about it!"

M: (She laughed) "Did he like cinnamon rolls in a foil pan with raisins in them? They have icing on them."

D: "Yes! His grandma used to get those for the kids."

M: "Did you two take a walk at sunset on the beach, you in a dress and he had his cargo pants, rolled up? His pants are wet at the bottom at sunset."

D: "Wow, yes! I have pictures."

M: "He said, 'Memories, sweet memories'."

Did someone make jelly?"

D: "Yes, his cousins have just sent delicious homemade jelly."

M: "I see, he has handwritten 'jam'."

D: "Yes, we have one now in the refrigerator that has a handwritten note on the jar, 'To my favorite cousin'."

M: "When Blake was there, did you make a really nice dinner?"

D: "Yes, we made a meal to match the $100 bottle of wine I had gotten as a gift."

M: "Cool. That's all I am getting."

In this reading, Michelle provided evidence that she was connected to Vern and that he was hanging around me. I no longer had questions about whether his soul had survived. I knew that he had.

CHAPTER 10: SACRED TRADITIONS

Journal Entry: Letter to Vern, April 22, 2009

Baby,

The process of packing up our home is agonizing. Each item has so many memories of something I can no longer have, something I cannot grow. I don't want to even get out of our bed in the morning. How do others do this? I have no choice, so I do what I must, but it is not easy. You have given me hope with all the evidence that you still exist. That is my fuel.

I got a call from your mom. She said that a friend of yours from the Ohlone tribe had called. He had just found out about your death. He said that you were a great man, and they would like to honor you and your family with a crossover ceremony at their Pow-Wow. Again, I welled with pride. You were a great man, and what an honor this is. I now know you will be able to enjoy it from where you are. I meditated after the call. I felt so close to you. I wanted to tell you in my mind about the honor you had received. When I was done, I swear I looked down and the feather you had found and placed on the window sill in the kitchen was down at my feet. How did it get there? Did you do that? I remember you used to say, "I am an Indian with a feather not a dot." If you did that, send more signs, and don't be too subtle.

Blake is out helping me get ready for the move. He knows the toughest thing I will do is move from the home we selected and made together.

I love you. I miss you. Keep the big signs coming.

Yours Eternally,
Bellows

There are very few things I like less than moving. It is third to dental work and public speaking. My friend Blake always seemed to come out of the woodwork to help me in times of need. He came to help me move and to help me heal. I loved him dearly for being my crisis intervention. I guess we did that for each other.

Blake and I were packing and talking the night before the crossover ceremony. He indulged me by listening to Vern stories all night in Vern's office. I had received the most amazing evidence the night before in my fourth reading with Vickie Gay. Blake was part of the story and was a witness to the original interaction, so I was very excited to tell him about it.

In this reading, I asked Vern if he had met his twin. Vern had a twin who did not make it to birth. I wondered if we kept connections with people that did not incarnate, or if that soul reincarnated. I wondered if we would recognize this kind of soul when we returned to spirit.

I replayed just the section of the fourth reading to Blake in which I asked the question, "Did you meet your twin?"

Vickie replied with a tone of confusion, "That's strange, in so many words, he said, 'I swallowed him whole', and he's making a chomping sound like Pacman."

This seemingly horrifying response puzzled the medium and me for moment. Alycia, my daughter, caught the reference immediately, and her jaw dropped.

The comment was actually in reference to a wise crack I had made to Vern and Blake six months prior. Vern was telling Blake (who is a twin) a story about being a twin. Vern said, "I always wondered what it would be like to have a twin," and then remarked that I am also a twin. Before Vern could finish his statement, I inserted a horribly sarcastic quip, saying, "Vern didn't think there was enough room in the world for two of him. Not wanting to share the spotlight, he ate his twin in utero."

As you can imagine, my tasteless joke invoked quite the response from Vern. He stood up and looked in disbelief. "What did you say?" He immediately walked across the room to my daughter and said, "Did you hear what your mean-spirited mother said to me?" He then dramatically declared, "What kind of person would say something like that!"

I felt a moment of pride by how shocked he was and the reaction I was getting. Vern and I developed this twisted sense of humor that only he and I enjoyed. It was a way of making light of an unjust world.

He said, "Your mother-in-law is going to be horrified by your behavior." And then he proceeded to say, "What's your mother's phone number? She needs to hear about this!"

I said, "Why tell your mom? She's the one who told me the story!" pa-dumpa!

Vern and I were always inappropriately sarcastic with one another. Our sarcasm was founded in our early days. It was the device we used to mask our feelings for one another, and it grew to a contest of who could out shock the other as adults.

It was very hard to shock Vern, I rarely got the pleasure. But this comment shocked him. My sarcasm had reached a new low. He then picked up the phone, called everyone, and told them about my poor joke in an effort to embarrass me.

At the moment of the reading, my oldest daughter was quick enough to catch it and play back for me while I was a little confused. My mind was not in the playful state we were usually in during our normal life together.

Blake was a witness to the story so, of course, he was amazed. He was also a witness to our brutal banter. I was finishing the story of the reading when all of a sudden, the room filled with the beautiful smell of gardenias. It was the sweet smell of Hawaii that we both knew well. It was where Blake and I met through a connection of Vern's. This scent was so strong we both took instant notice.

I said, "Do you smell that?"

"Yes," he replied, "Gardenias."

We both got up and looked for the source of the aroma. If we walked two feet away in any direction, we couldn't smell it. I walked outside to see if anything was lying at the door. I looked all around and there was nothing. When we returned to the room, the spot where we were sitting still had the beautiful fragrant smell. Was the aroma nothing more than random cells in the universe joining to form one of my favorite floral scents? We couldn't explain the source, so we chose to credit it to the magic of Vern.

The scent of gardenias reminded me that Vern used to bring me fresh-cut flowers. He would put them together in a beautiful way, or sometimes it would be just a single, glorious flower. I would feel his love pouring off of it. The girls at work thought I lived an enchanted life. After a visit I could hear the whispers, "Who was that masked man?"

I would giggle, knowing that our private life was far from perfect. But, at the core of our relationship was an undying love and devotion. I imagined the world would be a much better place if everyone took time to show simple appreciation. Everyone's cup would be running over. I knew mine was, but it wasn't because my life or relationship was problem-free. No, so far from it.

If I could do something a little better the next go round, I would express myself and my love for others more with simple gestures. A signed card: "I am so happy that you're in my life." Or even just, "Thinking of you," just like my love did for all he loved. I wish I would have learned this from him much earlier.

Any time I see a couple looking past one another in a malaise of boredom, I want to shake them and say,

"Hey, if you only knew this opportunity to connect could be gone tomorrow, you would not squander it."

Simple gestures can keep it all fresh. I bought Vern his cologne. I selected it for its clean, fresh, spicy scent and its beautiful sleek packaging, which reminded me of him. I spent a few weeks searching for the just right cologne. It was thought and care that counted. He could have selected his own cologne and then told me what to buy, but it's special when it comes from your lover's heart. I want to tell lovers all over the world to take the time, especially when you aren't feeling it, to do something special to bring it all back.

I went to the crossover ceremony with all the loving memories in my mind. I was aware that Vern would feel them.

Journal Entry: Letter to Vern, April 24, 2009

Mascorro my love,

The crossover ceremony is tonight. Your friends and family will be honoring you. I get so lost for words when people want to know how I am doing. I am so happy to know we are still connected, but I also miss our physical time together. I want to share with everyone how your spirit lives on very strong and that you are actively with us. But, most sort of give me the "Oh, ok." Give me strength to make you proud.

Yours eternally, Darcy

When we arrived at the crossover ceremony, the air was filled with the smell of sage smoke. There were hundreds of people dressed in Native Indian regalia. It was spectacular. I saw feather headdresses, boots, beads, colorful skirts, and beautiful jewelry made of bone, nuts and stones. There was face and body paint and the sound of the drums beating in synch with the heart. I was mesmerized by the fire, the sounds, and the sights. I could feel my thoughts being taken away. It was almost hypnotic.

Vern's mom, Henri, stood out in a crowd. She was strong, radiating with light filled healing energy. She still stood as a pillar of strength, but now she had an ever-present sadness behind her eyes.

Henri was dressed in a beautiful buckskin leather dress. She had turquoise silver native rings on all of her fingers. During the ceremony, she did a dance for her son. It was so moving. I could see Vern's tears streaming down in my mind's eye. I did not know how she did it, but she found the strength to dance and honor her son. The sound of the drums was hypnotizing. It was a six-hour mystical ceremony of dancing, drumming, chanting, and fire. All dedicated to my love. I felt awe and reverence; it was mesmerizing. When they chanted into the fire, the smoke seemed to plume in different colors.

That night, we returned to Vern's parents' home—the home Vern grew up in. I pulled up to the side of the house on the street just outside of Vern's childhood room. I had to stop because two feet away from the car, on the street, sat a white dove on the curb. I looked to my friend Blake and I said, "Do you see what I see?"

"Yeah, I see a dove."

Neither one of us could believe our eyes: a white dove, a symbol of peace, sitting on the street outside

Vern's childhood bedroom! Any other place I would have pulled up, we would not have found this dove.

Just then, Henri and Mike walked up and immediately noticed the dove. They moved toward it, and the thing just sat still, not flying away like you would expect of a wild bird.

I asked, "Is it injured?"

Henri picked it up, and Mike inspected it, "It doesn't look injured."

The kids gathered around and started calling the bird 'Vern'. Mike was perplexed. He didn't know what to make of this. In his thirty plus years of living at his house, he had never seen a white dove hanging about. Mike spent several hours a week in his yard and in his garden. If he said this bird was not indigenous to the area, I knew that was true.

Mike left for a minute to find a cage he had built for the injured animals Vern used to bring home as a boy. They placed the bird in it. At no point did the bird try to escape, nor did it appear uneasy about all the human contact. The kids, Henri, and Mike made sure the bird was fed and watered. The miracle dove did eat and drink, proving that it didn't seem to be injured.

Now I thought to myself, "What if one of the family friends bought a dove and placed it on the street or the front porch? Would placing it in the street be the smartest place? It was 1 AM. We had stayed with the tribe until they were ready to pack up. What are the chances the bird would be calmly sitting on the street for hours awaiting our arrival?" The other conflict was—a friend would know that Henri and

Mike don't normally go out to the street or the front porch when they come home. Normally they would pull their car into the garage in the backyard and enter the house from the back door. Henri and Mike rarely ever entered the house from the front and never pull up on the street. Chances are they would never even notice a bird in the street or on the front porch, if that was the original location. I only pulled up to the street because we were going to stop for a minute to figure out tomorrow's plan before heading to the hotel. Even guests usually parked in the backyard.

That bird, if left by a friend, would have been sitting there for several hours. Even if the bird was purchased and placed there, which I do not believe it was, that bird waited for the family and was in a spot where we all noticed—quite remarkable in and of itself. The unexplainable coincidences were starting to add up.

Henri and I together released the dove a few days later. We both knew the magical dove had a big purpose and should be released. As we released it, it left us each a feather. The act of leaving the feather for us also seemed miraculous. In the Native American tradition, the feathers symbolize many things. But most appropriately, they symbolize spirit communication and wisdom of life beyond earth. The dove flew to the balcony and turned toward us and perched. He looked at us for a few minutes then went to a higher perch, did the same thing, and then flew away. We figured the dove was on his way to help other families on this journey.

Mike and Henri asked the chief what he thought about the dove. He was surprised and said that it was very good omen. I looked up what the sign of the dove meant both in Christianity and in Native American tradition. Here is what it said:

The Dove Totem by Zahir Karbani
http://www.manizone.co.uk/dove-totem-a-41.html_

The skies will never see a more peaceful and graceful creature than the Dove. This animal has been respected and revered throughout the ages by ancient and modern Indian tribes and their Shaman. These tribes who are so connected to the elements and the Earth understand the true influence these creatures' possess. They are diplomatic, legendary animals that own many admirable virtues.

The Dove represents the feminine power of giving, prophecy, and the hope a new beginning. The Dove shows and reveals the veils between the spiritual and physical worlds. The Dove shows up in many legends and lore. They were the totem of Aphrodite the Goddess of Love, and they bore the ambrosia from the Goddesses which kept Zeus immortal, they are the symbol of sexual passion in India. The flock of doves called the 'Seven Sisters' in Greece is thought to be the daughters of Aphrodite. Sophia, The Goddess of Wisdom, in the Mediterranean, is said to have descended upon animal vessels as the form of a Dove. In Mexico the Dove is seen as both a Love Goddess and a Madonna. The Hebrews see the Dove as a symbol of peace and purity.

It was the Dove which returned to Noah's Ark to tell all aboard that land was found, in the Dove's beak was an olive branch, which was the symbol of peace. It is believed that the Dove's nature is so pure that even Satan himself cannot shape-shift into its form.

Doves, like many species of birds, breed and nest in pairs, they mate for life and build their nests, protect their territory and raise their young with their partners. The males as well as the females produce a milk-like substance, called 'crop milk' to feed their newborns with. Both parents take responsibility for the hatching and care of their offspring. The males will sit on the eggs during the day while the females take over the task at night. Both take responsibility for the guarding of their nest. The Dove occurs worldwide but their largest variety is in Indo-Malaysia.

The Magnificent Dove Totem possesses the following virtues:

Love, gentleness, new ideas, purity, sexual energy, intimate relationships, creativity, peace, family values, centered calmness, tranquility, support, assistance, new relationships, peaceful transition from difficulty, powers of the feminine, friendship.

The Dove animal totem is a strong spirit indeed and its magical properties are one of the most influential of all animal totems. Love, understanding, martial happiness and balance, peacefulness, and so much more can be integrated into the spirit of the possessor of this magical pearl and the Dove totem.

Journal Entry: Letter to Vern, April 29, 2009

Mascorro,

The dove that you sent was no ordinary dove. It was adorned with feathers all the way down to its talons, more like a hawk. It was a great handsome dove. It looked like it was wearing feather boots like the natives wear during their ceremony. Symbolically, the dove very much represented you: handsome, fearless, wise and graceful. As far as the Christian belief under which I was raised, I do remember the dove being a symbol of a peaceful crossover. I remember after the floods when Noah sent the dove to find land, the dove brought back an olive branch indicating it had found land and it was time for a new beginning. Is that what you were trying to tell me?

I can't explain all of this, but I know it is not just coincidental. Some people might say these are ordinary things that you haven't noticed until you looked for it, and you are placing meaning into things that are not there. The dove is hard to ignore. How does one read into a peace dove arriving at your home after a sacred ceremony, resting on the street where I happen to pull up? The thing I don't understand is if we humans, or spirit beings, can do this type of thing, why don't we do it more often? If we are part of some awesome creational force, why did we allow this to happen to us and why do we not retain the knowledge from our spirit incarnation?

Some have stated theories that we make contracts to learn lessons and that this was a contract we made. Interesting theory. How truly sadistic would we have to be to agree to this? I know I would never do this to you and would not sign up for this for myself. Why did we spend a lifetime waiting for one another? Waiting for the time to be right? Always in love, but tucked away for whatever reason. We were trapped making mistakes left and right, not focused on what truly matters, never feeling peace until we finally got together. We finally get it right, we are both the happiest we have ever been, and in an instant it is all taken away. I have to ask the question, why? I now have to return to the state of longing and this time my longing is for what I now cannot have in this lifetime. I hope when you talk to God or the elders you will ask why. Ask them to please help us understand.

The only sense I can make of this is that we signed up for this adventure which came with the good, the beautiful, the bad, and the ugly. Baby, still I have to be grateful for the ride we had. What will my new beginning be in the bottom half of this life now without you, my biggest of passions?

Eternally yours,
Bellows

CHAPTER 11: GHOST BUSTERS

After I received one personal phenomena or experience after another, I decided to objectify some of my research. I needed to put myself in situations where I had no investment in the outcome. Michelle, my new psychic medium friend, was the lead psychic investigator on the Central California Paranormal Investigators team, so she invited me to become part of her team.

Michelle put together a team of four intuitives whose main job would be to accompany the CCPI scientific investigators on investigations where paranormal activity had been reported. When Michelle invited me to be a member of the team, she said I would start as a trainee. Michelle believed the experience of feeling spirits other then Vern would help me get more confident with my ability.

I was a little fearful of the unknown, so I prepared for my first investigation by talking to Vern and praying to Mother Mary. When I was child, I often prayed to Mother Mary or Jesus after a nightmare and the images went away and allowed me to go back to sleep. I said to Vern, "Okay babe, don't hang me out to dry here, you better have my back." And, of course, he always had my back, so I felt duly protected. Of course, this could be mind over matter, but it doesn't matter if it gets the job done. My most recent experiences had definitely opened my mind to the possibilities. I felt well guarded going in. After all, who was going to mess with my strong man standing guard next to me?

Investigation 1: Sierra Sky Ranch

We went to an old lodge in the mountains outside of Yosemite in Oakhurst, CA, called the Sierra Sky Ranch. It was a rustic lodge that seemed like it was over one hundred years old. This is where I met Central California Paranormal Investigators' founder Jackie Meador. She covered the basic investigating protocols with the teams. She was very calm, and I felt comforted by her discerning logical mind and tactics. I did not picture her screaming or psyching anyone out; on the contrary, she was very level-headed and analytical.

We wanted our attention to stay focused on capturing phenomena. Jackie said it was important to keep quiet and that if you make sound or movement to report it out loud so that when we listen to the evidence we know what it is. We were split into groups and told that no one should stray from their group.

She then explained the tools of the trade. First was an EMF meter, an electro-magnetic field meter used to test power lines. It can allegedly measure spirit energy which creates electrically charged moving objects. Then there was a sensitive voice recorder that can detect sounds below the human ear range to capture EVP—aka electronic voice phenomena. And finally, there was an infrared camera that can capture images in the dark.

The EMF meter measures the strength of electromagnetic currents. It is thought that our spirit form is dense in electromagnetic energy. In order to establish there are no false readings, the investigators get a baseline reading of all areas of a room before the team enters. Each group had four to five physical phenomena investigators and one psychic medium. The medium could get impressions that could be investigated with the equipment of the investigators.

I was in training, so I got to learn from Michelle, a developed medium. Michelle had investigated the place previously, so she knew some of the history and names. She acted as teacher and pointed out areas she felt an orb or a spirit could be captured on the camera. She was pretty good at calling out when and where to shoot. I would say her accuracy was somewhere around 80-90%.

I didn't get much in the way of feelings or impressions; I was too busy observing others. Our team didn't get any action until near the end of the investigation. Upon entering room #9, I felt like I wanted to try and ask some questions to any potential spirits in the room. The scientific investigators took baseline readings and found no anomalies from the EMF meter. We put the EMF meter in the center of the bed, and I went and sat on the bed.

The team shot pictures as I sat down to ask questions. I got a chill as I was sitting down. The voice recorder was turned on and I stated to the air, "We are here to discover if there is life after bodily death, we would appreciate any help you could provide us in obtaining evidence. If there are any spirits in the area or room, please help us know by touching this meter in the middle of the bed. When you touch it with your energy, all the lights will light up and let us know you are here."

All eyes in the room were on this little device with five lights. If it lit up all five lights, it meant there was a very strong electromagnetic signal. We were told this was ghost energy. After a few seconds, the lights started to light: one, two, three, four, and five, and it turned green. I got excited by the prospect but tried to temper myself. The cameras started flashing as other investigators took pictures. Someone said, "I got an orb above your head."

I continued talking to the air, "You can help us by making the meter move in a pattern. Make the lights light up all the way to the top once for no, twice for yes. When you answer a question, it proves there is something intelligent behind the phenomena of the EMF meter lighting up."

I then proceeded to ask questions.

"Are you a man?" The meter lit up twice and stopped. Yes.

"Is this your home?" One light and stop. No.

"Do you have good memories here?" Two lights. Yes.

"Are you from this time?" One light. No.

"Are your friends still around?" One light. No.

The meter proceeded to light up at the end of each question. It seemed we were getting an intelligent response to our questions. It only lit up on inquiry. I was getting goose bumps before starting the questions.

After an investigation, the investigators review and report all evidence experienced and document it. The sound person is supposed to listen to amplified sound and watch the sound waves using mixing software on the computer. Evidently, a spirit's voice is so low we can't normally hear it with our ear just as we can't usually see the low emitting light orb. I anxiously awaited the results that would be revealed when we all came together for evidence review.

One of the student investigators had captured an orb as I was sitting down on the bed. The student took two pictures five seconds apart. The orb was only in one, proving it wasn't dust. I was, overall, thrilled by the results of my first investigation: orb photo and EMF meter responses but the coup d'état happened when team 4 got a class A EVP.

I could hear that team entering the room next door while we were setting up ours, one of the investigators reported feeling the temperature drop which is a recognized sign of spirit being present. As the team was entering the room, one of the investigators said, "Is everybody in?" Upon playback, a reply came in that sounded like a distorted radio. The voice asked, "Can we come in too?" It was crystal clear. I was there for the event live so I knew this was not a manipulation. I couldn't believe my ears: I listened to it over and over. It is very rare to have such a clear communication captured, but even rarer to be able to personally verify that these people were not interested in fabricating evidence.

Another team asked in their EVP session, "Are your friends still here?" The response was clear, "They are all gone now." An intelligent response is hard to argue with. A skeptic would say they don't hear it. All I want to say is don't put such a stake in being right. We humans are wrong all the time. Consider a new discovery as cause to explore more.

How did this happen? If spirits can do this, why can't we hear them more often? Can we hear only spirits who have not yet crossed over? Why can't I hear Vern?

One theory is that trapped souls or any souls who, for whatever reason, decide not go to the light are the ones we can hear and that can physically move things. They are the earthbound spirits. In my readings, all the mediums said that Vern had crossed over 'to the light'. Is that why he doesn't move stuff around me in an obvious way? Or is it simply because we don't take the time to notice? Another theory is that it takes a lot of energy to manifest and move something physically, so they can't do this on command. So many questions, too few answers.

Investigation 2: The Jeffrey Hotel

As I drove through endless miles of rolling farm lands to my next investigation, I was left wondering, "What on earth could be out here?"

I could regularly be found talking to Vern in the car, a spot where I could be alone in my insanity, as others perceive me talking on the phone. I asked out loud, "Okay baby, what's out here?" I had thoughts of the Wild West, notorious outlaws living in the town, the natives enslaved. I felt Vern saying, "They were unkind to my people, there was much suffering at the hand of the invader, warfare. A time in the town that was male-dominant."

I thought of a woman stepping off the stage coach: British or Scottish. I made up a story of a love triangle between this woman and the owner of the hotel and the banker. I got the name 'Thomas' for the banker; I got names 'Marie, Elizabeth and George.' I got a fire-destroyed town. I asked, 'How does it start?' I got lightening. I felt Vern telling me that the other side of his heritage was also early settlers which were Mexican. Now, one might say that this would be obvious history for California. I grew up in Minnesota; I knew nothing of California history. I was heading to the middle of nowhere, the middle of farmland close to Yosemite. I really didn't even have a clue we were headed to gold country.

I still felt no vivid vision or intense feeling. I would get a blurb, jot it down, get another idea, and write it down. Michelle taught us to try and meditate and write down what we get before an investigation. She was so advanced, or naturally gifted, she could almost, on command, remote view or astral travel to the site before she got there. Michelle got a tour of the hotel in her dream the night prior. She saw the hotel decorated in period fashion, she saw wallpaper in the dining room, and in the parlor she saw Victorian furniture. When we compared notes, she described the same lady I saw as the Inn Keeper also stepping off the stage coach.

When we met up with the others, we all picked up on the Inn Keeper—the same lady, same description. Michelle described and then sketched the Inn Keeper.

Someone very proud and proper, she oversaw all matters of the hotel.

Michelle said she got the impression that the ghost fixes the silverware to a traditional English set. She also said her guides told her Room #8 was going be hot with activity.

Imagine my surprise when we were assigned Room #8 without asking for it. I was very excited, and just a tiny bit afraid, of what 'a lot of activity' would look like, but I knew my man would not let any harm come my way. I never underestimate the element of surprise, being startled can create hysteria. The CCPI team always kept calm, which made for better investigation and no mass hysteria. The investigators were mature; they had debunked many cases drawing logical conclusions, but they had also seen enough unexplainable paranormal activity to know it exists. They were not quick to call anything paranormal.

On our way to dinner, we walked through the traditional dining room. It was like stepping back in time. In fact the wallpaper was green and appeared like what Michelle had described before our arrival. We had dinner in the old saloon. The antique smell, all old woodwork; this place is where legends of the Wild West were made. You can almost hear drunken old cowboys arguing. Five of us shared a table, and we were all excited. Salo started to tell us what she was getting psychically. As she was tuning in she gazed upward.

Dr. Salo Stanley, a chiropractor, sound therapist, artist/musician researcher, and psychic medium had just joined our team. This was our first full investigation together. Salo is a petite little dynamo. She said esoteric things like they were fact; she said them as though everyone else could see them just like she did. She's a super smart lady, able to explain in layman's terms some of the physics of the universe.

As we were dining, Salo gave us the spirits' view of the event. She felt notorious characters getting drunk and rowdy. She described the scene in vivid detail like it was in front of her now: "There's a man with a beard and moustache, he is tall and he is sitting next to a shorter guy with black hair. They were arguing, but they stopped when we stepped in. Five ladies in the bar isn't a usual sight: all eyes are glued on us." Salo said they were talking about vigilante justice and a hanging tree, which turned out to be across the street from the hotel. She said she felt both John Muir and Teddy Roosevelt had stayed in this hotel. She asked if there was a Chinese owned business next door.

Salo said, in a matter of fact tone, "The ghosts are a little frisky tonight, I felt one just touch my breast." Jen laughed and said she could feel the old miners had been in the gold mine too long. Jen was the other psychic investigator on the team. Jen was a feeler who could pick up the emotion in the room so powerfully that sometimes it overtook her. Her type of psychic is called a sensitive because her personal state could be affected by the energy of the people in the room. Jen was also a natural healer—very pure in her intention to help others, but sometimes her empathy would actually hurt her physical body.

I laughed at the supposition of horny ghosts. I was not nearly so tuned in that I was picking up on the vibe. Later in the evening we got a couple of shots of orbs on the ladies' breasts, including mine. I realize this is not iron-clad evidence, but very coincidental indeed. I am aware that nobody can prove some of these impressions. But it begins to seem more plausible when you align the fact that two of our psychic investigators were getting this vibe, and then we get physical evidence of an orb over a breast.

I could feel the thick air, but I still didn't get any vision. I wondered how they did that. If only I could receive messages from Vern with such clarity.

After dinner, we headed up to the room to get ready for the investigation.

Investigations were usually done at night. At night you can capture better orb shots, but that is not the main reason. There is stillness after the commotion of the day settles down. This is a time when we can listen and not be influenced by too much physical stimuli. This sort of stillness is required to recognize anything unusual.

The Psychic unit met in Room #8, and began preparing our equipment. We all felt a little a buzz—the room was so charged everyone could feel it, including me. Michelle said, "I think we have visitors". Salo said they were from the saloon.

We all saw something fly by out of the corner of our eye from one side of the room to the other. We started to point and shoot with our camera. Almost every time an orb was found in the shot at the predicted trajectory of the energetic force. It happened repeatedly with different cameras and different spots in the room. We were all enjoying the interaction.

Salo turned on all of her equipment. She had an EMF meter, an EM pump, a digital audio recorder, and a video camera. She started asking if the gentleman from the bar had joined us, and she told them they could tell us by going near the EMF meter or by trying to speak into the recorder. Just as she requested, the lights all lit up on the EMF meter, indicating an unexplainable spike.

Salo then thanked the spirits for showing they were here and started to explain what we were doing here. She said that we were collecting evidence, hence all the gadgets, and they could help us by rapping, tapping, moving things, and talking into the gadgets. Then, all of a sudden, the door opened on its own in a very controlled manner. We all calmly looked at each other. I began to nervously chuckle not sure how to feel about it. I recall addressing Vern inside my head, "OK Babe, you better be here by my side to protect me."

Jen started looking around the door and feeling for any air vents up, down, and all around the door on all sides. She placed the door in the same position and jumped up and down. She ran down the hall to see if she could get it to move. She came back in and said she couldn't find anything creating a draft or motion that could have moved it. So we all asked if the spirit could do that again. Salo thanked the spirit and explained we would love to get the evidence on camera and would he or she kindly do it again.

We all stared at the door intently for a couple minutes. We were just about ready to turn our attention away when the door started to slowly open again. We got it on tape. We were all thrilled. Michelle was snapping pictures as the door opened, and lo and behold she captured an orb at the doorknob.

The rest of the night yielded plenty more evidence but none as clear as the door opening on command, twice. We received many intelligent responses to questions on the EMF meter in front of a dozen people. We also got intelligent responses to questions on the spirit box.

The spirit box was built by Salo. She was working on what she coined a 'telephone booth to the other side'. Her creation was based on a Frank's box design—a radio that scans radio stations at a very fast rate. Salo's design consisted of a few modifications in the circuitry, scan rate, and of course, the most important ingredient was intent. Jen asked the spirits if there was anything the four beautiful women in the room could do to help them. The spirit box quickly stopped on the word SEX. I said, "Hey, speak for yourself. I am not part of that offer." We all laughed. Salo was sensing and talking about the amorous males all night. Now, I don't know how to feel about these horny ghosts, but it was pretty compelling to witness physical proof.

When I watch ghost shows, I am rarely impressed by what's captured. Contrarily, I was very impressed by what I witnessed, and maybe that's what it takes for most people. The psychic team was really tuned in that night; we got an amazing number of hits on the psychic read of the place. The history of the hotel was revealed at the end of the trip. We were validated with names including President Roosevelt and John Muir being guests at the hotel, the Chinese owned business next door, the enslaved Indians, and the present day moving of the silverware. The names of the people who owned and built the place were Elizabeth and George. During our interview with Jackie, the CCPI leader, she asked the group if we got anything archeological in this town and Salo reported that her guides were telling her it was a wooly mammoth. This startled Jackie as she wasn't expecting a fast and totally accurate response. Michelle also did an amazing drawing of Mrs. Jeffery, the Inn Keeper, prior to us finding a picture. Once we found it was a match.

We did not ask whether the silverware was moved, it was volunteered by hotel staff. I felt completely amazed by the whole weekend and the evidence it presented.

I only did an occasional ghost investigation after that because I was shown what I needed to learn. I learned that spirits can hang around places they knew in their physical lives, and they can manipulate energy in this plane to move things and to say things. Why some do, why some don't is like asking why do some people here in the physical move away from the place they grew up in, and why do others stay around one place their whole lives. It's not a mystery, it's a choice. I believe it's free will. I believe our spirit also has free will.

I am often asked if ghost investigating is creepy. I always say no, not for me. I wasn't interested in a scary experience; many people that investigate are interested in finding scary things. Some do it as a form of thrill seeking. That was not my agenda, and therefore I did not find it. I took actions not to get involved in anything malevolent. I do believe what you seek or what you put your thoughts and energy into is what you will mostly find. But, I also know there are chaos and things not in our control. Therefore I judiciously continued my research, never losing sight of the purpose which was and is finding and keeping connected to my beloved Vern.

Journal Entry: Letter to Vern, June 2, 2009

My Love,

I constantly think about how much more exciting and fulfilling all these new experiences would be if you were here experiencing things beside me. We discovered everything important and sacred together. I was so lucky to have someone to validate my experience, it amplified it. You would always make me laugh with a sarcastic quip or make me think with a soulful observation. I think about what you would say if you were standing next me at the Jeffrey when the door opened on its own. I can picture you being very calm and matter of fact on the outside and, depending on your mood, asking the spirit to leave or to come in and have a beer. The supernatural never seemed to shock or scare you; you expected things of nature that we don't understand. It was a knowing inside of you.

I have so many questions. If a spirit can manipulate things why can't or don't you open doors when I am thinking about you? What are the rules? How do you leave me feathers? Is that a report coming from where you are or something you move here? How did you send the family the dove, or me the butterfly? When I ask direct questions like this from the mediums I don't always get answers. I can tell direct questions like that take them out of passive receiving to their own brain. I don't know if it's because you can't answer those questions. Are there mysteries not meant for mankind to understand?

What I miss most is pondering it all together. You were so courageous you always helped me jump hurdles I might be afraid of. I just know you want to call me up as badly as I want to call you and tell me all the things you've seen and learned. Don't worry, baby, I won't stop trying to make these connections with you. It seems we understand very little in this life about what's possible, much less understand the vastness of infinity and all the possibilities of life beyond what my two eyes can see.

CHAPTER 12:
AN EVENING WITH SASQUATCH

Journal Entry: Letter to Vern, June 5, 2010

Darling,

Michelle stopped by today we went to the renaissance faire but before we went I got your message loud and clear. I am so glad you can continue to tease me from the great beyond. Michelle as I am sure you are aware asked me why you would be showing her Bigfoot.

I laughed nearly as hard as you did when the topic came up last with your godmother Lena. I was laughing so hard it made her laugh, she then said, he first presented an image of Bigfoot and I am thinking are you showing me Bigfoot? Why? That could not possibly have meaning to Darcy.

Then he showed me him laughing and pointing at a man using a wooden bigfoot foot imprint on a broom handle and planting the prints in the ground all around to give the false impression Bigfoot was there.

Are you kidding? I said, I shook my head, that's my guy poking fun at me from the other side. Of course there is a very funny story surrounding Bigfoot. Vern used to talk to his godmother almost every night and they would talk about anything just like two old hens.

Anyway I overheard them talking because Vern had her on speaker phone and she said, "Ahh Miho! Last night in the middle of the night I heard Bigfoot scream! Three times!"

Vern chuckled and said, "WHAT! you heard what?"

"Yeah Miho! I am not lying. I could smell the stench the scream was not like anything you have ever heard before."

When Lena was story telling with Vern her Latina accent would become very thick and Vern would mirror it back. Their discussion was very animated, with hands flying and the whole bit. "Oh! Neeena! he said back in a drawn out way, "How did you know it was bigfoot?"

"I knew Miho! I knew," then Vern started busting out laughing.

"Nina, I don't think it was Bigfoot, it was probably a wolf, just then he noticed I was listening and he said, "Darcy, Nina thinks she heard and smelled Bigfoot." he roared his biggest laugh.

In the midst of Vern's hysteria, I replied as straight and earnest as could be, "I believe her."

He looked at me with one of his eyebrows arched way up, "Oh you do, do you!"

"Yes I do! I have also witnessed bigfoot." I said with a calm, dead pan expression.

Vern just about fell off his chair in laughter. if he was hysterical before he was beyond now. "Oh! so both my wife and my godmother have seen Bigfoot and I am just learning this now. When did you see Bigfoot?" he taunted.

"When I was four I saw bigfoot out my window and you can ask my mother as she bore witness." "Oh now this beyond my wildest dreams, my mother in law has also seen Bigfoot?"

"No, I didn't say that, but she saw the evidence!" I said as I glared at him for contesting my truth.

"When I was that young we lived in a house located right next to the woods in Minnesota. That night it was in the middle of winter. I heard something at the window next to my bed so I looked up and it was Bigfoot."

Vern looked at me with a twisted smile, "Oh?"

I continued, "So I was paralyzed with fear. There was an outdoor street light that illuminated the darkness so I can clearly remember the features, and when I saw it looking in my room I froze like a deer, so I slowly turned away like I didn't see him and faced the wall."

"Oh, ok darling I'm sorry you had a nightmare when you were a kid. Why don't you and Nina console each other on your Bigfoot scares?"

"Hmmm!" I said, "Lena, I believe you and I know my mother can attest that there were tracks in the backyard left in the snow the following morning when I told her about it, it was no nightmare."

Vern actually did call my mother once I hung up with Lena, and my mother did verify that she saw the tracks. She also said she was more fearful that it was some weirdo dressed in a Bigfoot suit than an actual sighting.

Michelle laughed and said, "Well that's a new one. This job has some unusual twists. I can honestly say I have never before encountered someone who has had a Bigfoot story, that is definitely unique evidence!"

____

Mascorro,

Darling please don't ever stop sharing stories with those that have that incredible gift to hear what we can't, it keeps those glorious memories alive!

Thank you my love , Yours eternal, Bellows

P.S. I told you Bigfoot was real, I am sure you know that now.

CHAPTER 13: SANDRA'S MAGICAL MYSTERY TOUR

My friend Michelle had introduced me to one of her medium friends in Los Angeles. I was going to be spending a couple of months with my in-laws until I found a place to work. The economy was terrible in 2009. I figured the space was needed to heal, so while I lost most of my earthly possessions and had no money to spend, I gained the clarity that none of it mattered in the wake of losing my love.

Sandra was a psychic investigator; she liked solving mysteries. She had a big network of Lightworker friends she would use to help collaborate with on cases. She was also a natural fit, someone I can see Vern and myself hanging out with. She was a beautiful Latina in her early 50s that looked like she was in her early 30s. She was funny, straight forward, outgoing, and seemed to enjoy life.

She was really into the laws of attraction. I could not agree completely with some of her beliefs, but it certainly is good for thought. She believed that at some level, you attract everything to you, including death and rape. While I understand what you give focus and energy to is what you will generally experience, I do not believe that we have control over everything through thought. We are sharing this space and time with others. How does the universe decide in a moment which thought to honor? I also believe we have many superficial thoughts that are not tied into agendas and are merely a passing wonder. The universal law, people believe when something bad happens to you it is something you attracted at a level you may not understand.

I can assure you that at no level did I want to lose Vern. I did sometimes fear my happiness would be stripped from me in some way, though I would not say it was central to my thought process. But on a rare occasion, I worried over things I could not control. Another friend, who was a past life regressionist, explained Vern and I's separation in this lifetime as my karmic lesson. She said I had many past lives where I was dependent on others; this life was to establish independence. This was hard for me to accept since I was independent from the cradle. I had clearly established independence in the forty years prior to Vern's passing so I didn't feel I would be taught independence from it. Rather, I actually made myself vulnerable to needing another and it was stripped from me. I wonder what the lesson was in that. Neither of the theories completely made sense to me. But I think both are intriguing theories and have some truths to them.

I still stand firm in my belief that this earth experience is a free will experience. I still maintain that once we left the garden, we were no longer under God's protection. It's like leaving your parents' house, and just like a parent, He is there to console and help heal when unfortunate incidents occur. When things go well, He is there to rejoice.

I very much enjoyed engaging in these discussions with Sandra and anyone that cared to. The exchange of ideas is always expansive if you open your mind to the exchange. Sandra was taking me on her magical mystery tour of Los Angeles It was a typical glorious sunny L.A. day, which is why so many people live there. Sandra's tour started out at the Self-Realization Fellowship Lake Shrine. It was an oasis in the middle of a busy city, an escape. This center was donated by Ghandi; it was created for a quiet place, a place to learn to connect to the Creator directly. Sandra suggested we walk through the path silently one time around. I was willing to try; the setting certainly deserved reverence. It felt like a church of God's creation, there were little waterfalls, a lake/pond with koi and turtles, swans, egrets, flamingos, ducks, tree birds singing all around. There were trees of all varieties, flowers in abundance, and statues that were symbols from religions all around the world.

In my silence, I felt sadness, reflection, warmth, and a moment of happiness and wonder. I imagined holding Vern's big, strong, protective hand. I imagined him lying down on the grass like we had done so many times before. I laid my head on his chest and he told me all the secrets of the universe he knew. I wondered, if I concentrated long enough, could I move from my imagination to a clairvoyant vision and actually get those secrets. My imagination only took me to the inquiry.

The next time Sandra and I walked through, we talked about our lives. Sandra was such a deep person. She shared a story about some of the physical signs she received when her mother died. She said, "Just learn to trust, Darcy, it is as simple as that."

"I have been wrong in my intuition before, how can I trust?" I replied.

"You were wrong in the ego and in the mind, not in the soul. Besides, it could be that you interpreted it wrong."

She gave me an example of how I might be getting it right but not getting what I expected. Maybe it wasn't wrong, maybe it was just a matter of a different perspective.

"Let's do an exercise right now," Sandra said. "Take a look around you and without naming this place, describe it."

I described the winding road and the rock canyon. Then she described the wild flowers alongside the road. She pointed out that we both described the same location differently and neither of us was incorrect. She said psychic phenomena come in many different forms. This, layered on top of the reader's current state of being and ability to separate her own bias from the message, makes for a delicate balance.

Our next stop on this healing drive was strangely familiar. I had been to this mystical place before. I remember driving through the area with Vern in Topanga Canyon just a year prior to his passing. We stopped at the very same restaurant Sandra pulled into; it was now called 'Inn of the Seventh Ray'. The restaurant was hidden from view because it was canopied by huge trees. It had seating outdoors, the sound of waterfalls, and the scent of jasmine. This was a place where God would go to eat. It was fantastic to be brought to a place of such significance that almost seemed like a dream from the distant past.

Upon entering the garden-like restaurant, we were surrounded by piped in soft music. Sandra seemed startled and jumped up suddenly. She said, "Darcy. Darcy, this is for you."

"What is for me?"

"Vern wants you to hear this song, shh! Listen."

We stopped, and I focused on the music. I heard four or five words but I couldn't make out the song. I kind of shrugged and felt a little frustrated for not being able to place it immediately. Just then the song coincidentally stops and starts over. This made Sandra's jaw drop as she looked at me excitedly. She obviously knew the song.

It was a beautiful, melancholy, melody; it brought tears to my eyes. I would normally not take the time to appreciate such 'sappy' music. Vern was much more romantic on the outside than I was. I used to tease him for listening to this type of music. But after losing Vern, I became the sap I teased him of being. I finally learned that being tough on the outside did not spare me from pain. At that moment, I let go of my cool exterior and cried as I listened to the whole song all the way through.

When it finished, Sandra patted my arm with comfort and said, "This is how he feels for you; he did that! He started the music over so you would hear it. Do you know the song?"

"I don't," I said, "but it sounded lovely. I was over taken with emotion."

"This is a song from that movie, Somewhere in Time, with Christopher Reeve about two separated lovers," she explained.

"Oh, I don't remember the movie, but the song seems lovely."

"Look it up, girl, it's very deep. He said he loved this movie and he wants you to watch it."

I went home that night and I looked up the song lyrics, such powerful words of love. I stared out the window with a longing that only those who have had the kind of love that filled that night sky with magic could imagine. The lyrics played through my mind over and over again.

The theme song to Somewhere in Time was by John Barry. The lyrics' main theme: none other than eternal love.

Journal Entry: Letter to Vern, June 8, 2009

My Love,

Part of me still feels it is not possible for you to manipulate energy to get me messages despite the too-coincidental nature of the dozens of signs you are sending me. I don't know why I cling to what I was taught. We are taught many things that are proven wrong later. Afterward, we all know the earth is not flat or that fire is not supernatural. I can hear you saying, "What do I have to do to get you to believe?" Darling, I do believe, I just feel stupid for not waking up before this and clinging so tightly to things that didn't serve me or us. Others still want to make me feel gullible for believing.

That song was so beautiful. Indeed there are other lovers that walk the earth that have felt what we have shared, and all this time I thought we were the only ones. I did not share my story immediately with our family because I thought they would think it silly just a strange coincidence; poor Darcy just seeing what she needs to see. I have shared many of the readings and even after the dove, some seem reluctant to accept the signs as the gifts they are.

Mike stepped into the room today as I was looking for work on the computer. He asked if I wanted to watch a movie that night. He was going to go to the library. I said, "Sure, sounds good. Are there any good movies at the library," I laughed.

"Yes we have been renting movies from the library for years, dating back to when Vern was just a boy," Mike said.

He continued, "I remember Vern watching this one movie over and over again when he was only twelve or thirteen. He made everyone that came over watch it with him. I swear he watched it at least ten times."

"Really? What movie was that?" I inquired curiously.

It was a movie about Something in Time with the guy who played Superman.

My jaw dropped in disbelief. I replied, "The movie with Christopher Reeve Somewhere in Time?"

"Yeah, that's it. He loved that movie. Have you seen it?"

"No, I remember it being too deep for me. I was too young to appreciate it, but you're never going to believe what I have to tell you about this movie and what happened to me two days ago."

I told him the story.

He didn't give much reaction, but I could tell he was processing it. I knew it helped inch him closer to knowing. The knowing I now have because of you. The knowing I want your mom to have.

That night I rented the movie, and my love—once again—you brought me to my knees. I couldn't help but laugh at myself. You were so romantic in spite of the bravery it took to be mushy in front of me. It was in your nature; you were 12 when you fell in love with this movie. I just shake my head wondering how difficult it must have been for you to reveal this side of you to me. Me and my tough, cool, Minnesota exterior, my sarcasm, and my defense to being vulnerable. It is difficult for me and my people to express in words such deep feelings; it's like opening the flood gates. The Germans and Swedes are good builders: we fortify that wall and hold in our emotions well. I hope my actions spoke in place of my words, but truthfully, you deserved to hear the words too.

The song lyrics, well, it was like they were written for us. I got a vision of that misty day in Golden Gate Park where we reignited our romance after so many years had passed. It was like coming home. That day was magical too. The fog was rolling in against the blue sky. You kissed me in public and had a stranger take our picture to capture that moment of unbounded joy.

I remember our giddiness. We acted like children—we went into the woods, you started stripping off your clothes. As panic moved over me, you said take a picture so you will never forget our day in Golden Gate Park. I screamed, "Get your clothes back on before someone comes!" I looked behind me and scampered a few feet in each direction to make sure nobody was coming. You laughed and said, "I will after you snap the picture".

Your free spirit rocked me to my core! I still have the picture and remember it fondly.

I listened to the song and watched the movie that you appeared to have sent, over and over this week, to relive those beautiful memories.

Thank you, my darling, for being vulnerable and honest despite my hard exterior, you softened me. This is just one of the gifts of freedom that you gave me. You opened my heart, mind, and imagination. You gave me freedom from my own personal prison, my own confining views and belief. How did you do that? You were and are so brave.

Yours Eternally, Darcy

The next time I saw Sandra, we were comfortable like old friends. She said almost shyly, "I've got to tell you something Vern showed me right before you came—but it's really embarrassing and I don't know how to say it. So I am just going to blurt it out: Was

Vern obsessed with the male anatomy a certain part and the size of it?"

I burst out laughing and nodded my head, "Yes! He told me all men were."

"Oh my god, Darcy, I was so nervous. I did not want to bring this up, but Vern said you would appreciate it. I didn't know how you would take it, but I had this friend who had created these t-shirts that had the giant male part I was referring to on it. I found one in a drawer this morning, and Vern popped in. He had this big laugh and he said, 'Give it to Darcy. She will know it's from me'."

I do know it's from him, he loved to embarrass me and others by speaking openly on topics where others did not dare tread. He loved it! He bought a tabletop art book with beautiful photographs of men's bodies, all with the common denominator of an out of natural scale male unit. He would take out his new purchase and show friends just to get a reaction and to embarrass me. I am sure he was also genuinely impressed and envious.

CHAPTER 14:
SIGNS, SIGNS, EVERYWHERE SIGNS

Journal Entry: Letter to Vern, June 12, 2009

My Love,

Your friend from college, Christine…her brother died unexpectedly. He got the flu and passed; he was only 30 years old. When someone you know dies, will you be there to greet them? I wish I could give the widow some comfort. I would let her know her lover will be there whenever she needs him, but I know at this stage it is very little consolation and a lot less than she needs not to miss the life she enjoyed, the one she created with him.

Your mom and I are going to go and help at the funeral. Your friends were so supportive with yours. I still don't know how to act in this situation, except to not try and make the grieving feel better or make it right. I know just to show respect and appreciation for the soul that has left the body.

I love you; I miss you and your body,
Bellows

The sky was deceptive the day of the funeral service. It was so blue and glorious; the temperature was a perfect 82. The funeral ceremony was outside. Vern's friend Christine spoke at her brother's funeral. She spoke of a traditional Mexican belief that after our deceased relatives are received happily in heaven the soul flies down on the wings of a butterfly to visit their loved ones and let them know they are safe. After the story, they released a few dozen of these beautiful butterflies and then they told the romantic story of Michael and his now widowed bride. Theirs was a story of love at first sight, or at least it was for Michael. He knew she was the one, which was much the same way I felt for Vern. The tears streamed down my face. I felt compelled to speak to the widow, a woman I had never met. I knew the hell she would endure, and I knew she would not yet be ready to hear about his consciousness surviving death. I just wanted her to know how sorry I was for her loss.

As I was waiting in line, crying for myself and crying for the young woman that would soon understand my pain, a monarch butterfly landed on my arm. I tapped Henri and said, "Look." She nodded and smiled. The butterfly sat patiently as I moved around and walked forward. It was at least ten minutes until we got to the front of the receiving line where Vern's friend and her family sat.

When I walked up to Christine, she said, "Well, it looks like we have a visit from my good friend today." She told her mom in Spanish that this was Vern's wife and mother, (everyone knew Vern) and then she pointed at the butterfly resting on my arm and said, "Vern is sending us a special sign today." She knelt down beside the widow and explained to her the gift of this butterfly visit.

"My friend, Vern, is sending us a message today from above," she said. As I hugged the family, the butterfly was not bothered by all the commotion; it sat patiently on my arm. Henri and I stepped off to the grass to soak it all in, and the butterfly remained for a couple more minutes. In those minutes, I imagined Vern greeting Christine's brother. Vern hugged him, put his arm around him, and started to introduce him. Vern was standing in an open veranda surrounded by tropical trees and birds in the back. The ocean was far off in the background. The light was very intense with a purple hue. He was in comfortable white cotton clothes, his shirt unbuttoned down to his abs. I clearly saw him barefoot; I saw the details of his feet. They looked freshly covered in sand. I came back to my surroundings.

That day I had my first clairvoyant experience. Some call it day dreaming, others call it visualization. I learned the difference between visualization and a clairvoyant vision. With a clairvoyant vision, you do not guide it, it seems to come to you with no input from you.

Only days after Vern's death, a hummingbird hovered outside of Henri's window as she did the dishes, the thoughts of her son still constantly at the surface. Henri took note of the hummingbird and told me about it that night.

The grand signs made me believe in the little signs. After the dove I started accepting the feathers that I had been secretly believing were signs. Vern had an expression that he used to describe his ethnicity, "I am Indian with a feather not a dot." In the first two weeks of his passing a feather he had collected seemed to magically move from the ledge in the kitchen to my foot on the couch after my first reading. They seemed to pop up when I was thinking about him. I started collecting some of them, though I didn't tell anybody of my collection because I thought they would find it silly.

Michelle had come over for circle and told me she saw a vision of Vern taking a pillow and ripping it in two and feathers flying all around. I had just picked up a white feather that looked like a big goose feather from an old fashioned pillow. I thought maybe this was Vern's way of validating I wasn't nuts for thinking maybe the feathers I was noticing were to remind me that he was around.

I told Henri about my feather thing, and wouldn't you know it, both trips we took together to memorialize Vern we found feathers in our path. One of the spots was an extremely bizarre spot for a feather. We had gone to the Getty museum in Los Angeles for what would have been our wedding week. Vern and I both had a great appreciation for the arts, so we felt this was a great spot to go. On the third floor, they had beautiful paintings, and the floor was made of an incredible marble. It was so spotless it glistened; you could eat off of it. We talked about the feathers as we were walking through the building, and we stopped to take in the beautiful work. Henri looked down and saw a feather at our feet. She picked it up and handed it to me, "How about that?" she said.

I replied, "Indeed. How about that?" I so badly wanted Henri to know her son was with us. Every sign compounded would help her understand for sure.

Early on, she was sitting in her living room thinking about her son and the dream catcher she had made started swinging, not just a little but pretty good. She quickly looked around to see if she could see anything else moving. After all, we live in earthquake country, but she saw nothing else swaying or shaking. She asked out loud if that was Vern and the swaying seemed to pick up. She thought about the fact that Vern had wanted her to make dream catchers. She knew it was him, but still had a glimmer of doubt because we were taught by men interpreting the bible that spirit communication was done only for evil purposes. It was sorcery.

How ironic, humans have taught us that the prophets who wrote the Bible were receiving messages from spirits. They were so bold as to call what they were doing sorcery. Oh, but they were anointed men... hmm I wonder how one would test that? There was no sorcery involved. I've received nothing but comfort and healing messages of love, definitely from a higher loving spiritual force.

Henri was not yet open to receiving a reading, despite all I told her. She said she was afraid that she wouldn't hear what she wanted to hear. I told her when she was ready I would see that she got a good medium. The last thing you want to do is send someone who desperately needs comfort to someone who is not connecting.

I wonder, if spirits can speak to birds and butterflies, why this hasn't become a common practice? Why don't spirits upon safe passage to the light send a butterfly or hummingbird to their spouse, parent, and child? Or do they? Maybe that is where the odd tradition stems from. Maybe we, in our busy modern lives, don't take the time to notice, so they don't bother. I cannot say, but I can say the many experiences that I had seemed more than just an odd coincidence, and when you add all them all up well it's simply miraculous and defies explanation.

CHAPTER 15: CONNECTING ACROSS THE POND

I was singing along and feeling the words from one my favorite songs, "Like a Stone" by Chris Cornell. The song seemed to be written for parted lovers that were stuck in different dimensions. He awaits his love with an agonizing loneliness. As Cornell sang he seemed to understand the longing of separated lovers and the loneliness that you feel. I wondered where he received his inspiration from. I needed someone to relate to. I knew the only person that could truly relate was Vern. For now, the only path to relating to him was through a medium. My trusted medium sources were starting to know my story which did not prevent them from a good reading, but it did make it a little harder not to fill in the details with preconceived notions. I was curious to see if there was cultural or location barriers to readings.

I found this wonderful medium on the web from the United Kingdom. Her name was Bernie Scott, and she was from Bristol. I was searching for physical demonstrations of mediumship through Google and found there is quite a lot of research on the topic in the UK. Physical mediumship is the practice of trying to physically manifest spirits. There are documented cases of spirits forming ectoplasm, a web-like substance that comes through a medium doing a sitting. That substance allows the spirit to use her energy. The ectoplasm is used for transporting objects from the other side called apports or forming physical matter to communicate. I was very interested to witness one of these readings. I found Bernie while searching for this very rare skill.

Bernie was not a physical medium. Rather, she was coined as an evidential medium and considered great by the physical medium I had read about. I was very curious as to what a reading would be like in a culture where gifts of spirits were a little more accepted. I had heard a few radio shows where the Brits seemed to accept spirit communication as part of our humanity a little more readily then we do as a whole. An evidential medium meant the reading would focus on providing specific evidence that would be unique enough to prove that their loved one was the person the medium was connecting to. I had done dozens of readings that provided general statements but very few were good at specifics. After I read the description of an evidential medium I connected with her on Facebook.

Bernie had bigger than life energy, just like Vern. She made me feel at ease instantly. She had a great laugh and talked confidently about what she saw. She was so warm, it was a comfort just to speak with her.

Bernie Scott's Reading

B: "I don't know who is drawing near, but I have to talk about your mediumship skills because I can actually see you doing this for yourself or for other people."

D: "Wow, I am actually studying."

B: "Darcy, they're making me feel like you need to meditate more."

D: "Yes, it is hard for me."

B: "You really need to work on going into the silence because they're making me feel like when you do meditate, you're making a big thing of it. Do you have some sort of ritual that you do?"

D: "Yes I do the grounding cords, and I do guided meditations and try to visualize without much success."

B: "They're making me feel you're doing some sort of big ritual. It's not necessary; just open in prayer and keep your mind blank. Don't expect to see anything. Nine out of ten times you won't see a thing. Stop comparing your experience with others. Are you trying to compare? The void, the silence, is the best place to be. Don't compare to anybody. Nobody can say how it should be for you."

D: (A confirming chuckle) "Yes, this is true."

B: "You have this wonderful healing energy about you. I don't feel you have trained in any modality; it is natural."

D: "No I haven't trained in healing at all."

B: "I know you sing while you do your mediumship, but you must sing other times as well."

D: "It's true that I sing while I do my mediumship. I get songs for people. I wish I could sing well, but usually it's for my ears only. I love music and find it very healing. I wish I could sing to entertain and heal, but I don't have the voice for entertainment purposes."

B: "I get the sense that your voice is very healing for people. Have you done any teaching, Darcy?"

D: "Yes, yes, I have."

B: "I have a gentlemen drawing close that is giving me thoughts that you have done teaching.

I'd like to say children but...I don't think it is children."

D: "Right, I teach at work. I'm a manager and I co-teach at the psychic development circle with an actual medium."

B: "That's great! As this gentleman draws near, I feel like he had a bad breathing condition right before he passed, like emphysema or lung cancer or pneumonia. Is this dad or grandad?"

D: "Yes, grandad."

B: "Did he live near you?"

D: "Yes, he did while he was alive."

B: "Now a lady is drawing near. Was she out of state when she passed?"

D: "I was."

B: (She chuckled at my contrary reply) "Yes, ok. Did she have trouble with her legs? Is it your gran?"

D: "Yes."

B: "You have felt her before."

D: "Yes."

B: "She has blown in your face recently and tried to communicate."

D: "Okay. Yes, I have felt that."

B: "In your circle, can you trust what you're getting a bit more?"

D: "Yes, I need to."

B: "Because she's making me feel like you are getting thoughts that you are not passing along. You're thinking, 'I might be wrong, so I am not going to say it'."

D: (Chuckle) "Yes. Exactly."

B: "Can I just say, we all go through the wrongs to get to the rights."

D: "Right."

B: "Our guides don't actually know what we are picking up 100% until it comes out of our mouth. When you say to the sitter, 'I am getting a sense of blah, blah, blah,' the guide hears it and then knows whether you got it right and will adjust next time accordingly."

D: "Okay."

B: "When you meditate, you won't necessarily get a lot of visions, Darcy. But when you're done, say, 'I saw X, I felt Z, I heard Y' out loud or in your head, so spirits gets a sense of what you got. That will help you leaps and bounds. Spirits will be working with you on something special. Are you working on something fantastic with spirits, Darcy?"

D: "Yes, a book."

B: "Is this book about your journey?"

D: "Yes, it is autobiographical."

B: (She laughs again) "Yes that is your journey. They are very excited about this."

Can you understand a younger man in spirit? A man that went before his time? I get all goose-bumpy. I suddenly felt him when you mentioned the book. As he comes in, he's blowing you kisses."

D: "Yes."

B: "He is saying, 'I love you'."

D: (I wince) "I love you, too."

B: "'I love you.'

Did he go quite quickly to the spirit world?"

D: "Yes."

B: "He is making me feel it was over in an instant. You didn't have time to, to say goodbye, did you, Darcy?"

D: (I whimper) "No."

B: "Alright, sweet heart. He has heard you say you love him a million times."

D: (I cry more).

B: "It reminds me of the film Ghost. I almost wanted to say, 'ditto'. Is there any significance here?"

D: "Yes." (I cry).

B: "Because he keeps going, 'Ditto. Ditto.'

Did he give you a ring?"

D: "My sister just gave me a ring two days ago for him. He was not able to before he passed. It was on his to-dos, and we were to be married."

B: (she interrupts) "Okay, I know because he said, 'you are my wife, you are my wife'." (Bernie gets overwhelmed with emotion from Vern.)

"He keeps taking me to a beach."

D: "Yes."

B: "Many great times there. I think he was quite well toned."

D: "Yes. Yes, he was."

B: "He was showing me that. Has your hair changed since he passed?"

D: "Yes, I went back to blonde from red as he wanted to be married with me blonde. He has seen me in every color."

B: "Well, he quite likes your hair."

D: "Good."

B: "What is the number six?"

D: "He died a little over six months ago."

D: "Did someone nearly drown in their own fluids? Is there a memory here of someone nearly drowning, like a lifeguard thing?"

D: "I don't know."

B: "He's making me feel it's you, it's symbolic. You nearly drowned in grief when he passed, and it is his hand helping you back up."

D: "Yes."

B: "Are you eating ultra-healthy right now?"

D: "Yes, I am living with his parents and they are health nuts."

B: "I feel like I am craving a burger. He wants you to send his love to his parents. Did you recently take out his picture and talk to it and kiss it?"

D: "Every day."

B: "He says this, 'This was love at first sight.' He's making me feel like this was love at first sight."

D: "It was!"

B: "I don't know if it's you or him with the really big eyes."

D: "I think his favorite feature was my eyes."

B: "Yes, he is showing me lovely eyes and lovely eyelashes."

D: "But it could have been him, he was striking."

B: "Oh yes," (she laughs) "I can imagine. I am feeling him here.

I know that his funeral was huge."

D: "Yes, 2,000 people."

B: "Why am I hearing drumming in the background?"

D: "His mom drummed for him at his funeral and at his crossover ceremony. They are Native American."

B: "I feel I have a white dove in my hands, and I want to let it go."

D: "Oh My God!" (I get chills) "After his crossover ceremony, we pulled up to the house Vern grew up in, and there was a white dove on the street outside his bedroom window. We believe he sent it. Three days later his mom and Mike put it in my hands, and I released it into the sky."

B: "The dove had his essence of spirit there. Okay, he was there. He was there for a reason, and it was from him. You need to know."

D: "Yes, I know; it was incredible."

B: "Darcy, I keep hearing him saying how much he loves you. I can feel it so strong. I don't think I have ever felt this bond before with a couple, to be quite honest."

D: (I break down) "Yes, it was very deep."

B: "Who has a little tattoo?"

D: "Alycia, my daughter, his stepdaughter, got a little tattoo on her wrist in honor of him."

B: "Oh God! Darcy, if you could see me, I have my hand around my wrist. Send his love to her, he is around."

D: "Yes."

B: "Did you dance in a dream with him?"

D: "I can't remember my dreams, sadly. It's all I want to do."

B: "When we are in grief, we sometimes block because our aura is so heavy. You will dance with him again, Darcy."

D: (I sniffle) "Hmm, good."

B: "Oh, he had a nice pair of legs, Darcy." (She laughs)

D: "He sure did."

B: "I don't know if he wore shorts a lot, but I feel like he did."

D: "Almost all the time, year round."

B: "Okay, I don't feel like the accident was his fault. I am seeing a really bright light coming toward him. Huge white light, and then I don't remember anything after that. I am blinded by the light."

D: "Another medium said the exact same thing."

B: "It's an intense white light. I can actually say that he didn't feel anything. Maybe it was spirit coming to get him; it's an intense blinding light."

D: "When you say that I remember something, there was actually a metal/chrome console around the shifting gear between the bucket seats in our car. This used to blind Vern while driving. In the middle of the day when the sun hit it just right, he would flinch when it hit him in the eye. He always use to bring a towel when he remembered, to cover it up. My last trip to Los Angeles, I rented a VW, which was our car. The console was chrome, and it blinded me. I remember how it used to irritate Vern. He said it was a major design flaw. I think he was trying to tell me this last month when I took the trip but I didn't put two and two together."

B: "Yes, that could be it, Darcy. Does someone have a recording of his voice?"

D: "Yes, his mom and I recently listened to his recording from his voicemail."

B: "The telephone, when you and his mom listened to it together, he was there with you.

I don't know if you lost weight, but he said don't lose too much weight."

D: "I have recently. I could lose more, but that is sweet of him to say."

B: "This is an English song you probably don't know that my guides are giving me because they help out in the readings, 'I love you because you understand me, every little thing I try to do'. These are words I had to give you because he really felt that you understood him and you knew how he worked."

D: "Yes, very much." (I cry a bit)

B: "Did you want to take your own life for a split second? You wanted to be with him."

D: "I have kids, so it's not an option. But I want to be with him, so it certainly crosses my mind, but not as an option."

B: "He said you have too much to do here. You are going to help a lot of people, and he is going to help you help them."

D: "Okay, as long as he is here." (I cry.)

B: "He is, Darcy, he is. Did your daughter like horses by any chance? I feel he is with her when she is around the horses."

D: "Yes she took lessons and worked at the stables last summer."

B: "Do you have a son?"

D: "No, but I have nephew he was very close to."

B: "Is he into bikes or is he getting one?"

D: "I don't know, I will ask."

B: "Vern is really conscious about the hazards on the road, and Vern wants him to be cautious but not to worry too much. Just keep his eyes on the road.

Have you been looking for your passport?"

D: "Yes! Does he know where it is?"

B: "He is showing me an overflowing drawer, so it fell behind the drawer, if that makes sense."

I want to go to one of your daughters, has one of your daughters had a photo shoot?"

D: "Yes! She isn't starring in it, she is helping to dress and organize the talent."

B: "Well, he is very excited about it."

D: "She is, too."

B: "He is very proud of her, you have very talented girls. And he said they always made him feel like part of the family."

D: "I think so, too."

B: "Were you together for eight years?"

D: "We have been in love for 25 years, but for one reason or another only came together a year and half ago."

B: "Did you start getting back together eight years ago?"

D: "Wow. Yes, now that I think of it. We both separated from our partners, and I moved in with him. We started casually talking about it from that point on. That was exactly eight years ago. We celebrated his 30th birthday the month after I moved in 2001."

B: "Okay. Who is planting a tree or a plant for him?"

D: "His stepdad, Mike, did."

B: "Is he painting a fence?"

D: "Yes, and he is painting the siding on the house right now. This is something Vern always wanted to do for them."

B: "Okay. That's great."

B: "Was he into herbal remedies?"

D: "Yes, he was. And so is Mike, his step dad, and his mom."

B: "Are you starting to get into that herbal medicine?"

D: "I was always interested in it when he talked about it."

B: "I feel this is something he is going to help you with later on...Who still has a pair of his shoes?"

D: "I have all of his stuff. I was looking at his shoes because we are moving, so I am packing."

B: "I feel like he didn't like wearing them very much, like he'd rather be barefoot or wear a pair of sandals."

D: "Yes that is very true." (I laugh)

B: "I just want to sing the song, 'You were meant for me, everyone tells me so'. You were meant to be together."

D: "I couldn't agree more."

B: "It's a shame you waited so long. I do feel, though, that there was always a strong tie between you two."

D: "Yes!"

B: "Always.

You know, do you have any links with Oregon?"

D: "His aunt, Thunderbear, lives in Oregon, as well as some cousins."

B: "He sends his love. Is there some sort of ceremony coming up, like two tribes coming together, like a feasting time?"

D: "Yes. I think his Uncle's tribe's Pow-Wow."

B: "Why does he show me a house being boarded up?"

D: "We are moving again."

B: "He wants you to think of this as a new beginning."

D: "He will walk your walk with you."

B: "Who has a June Birthday?"

D: "Alycia."

B: "He has video footage that he wants you to find."

D: "Oh cool, I have to find the power cord."

B: "Did you think you felt him in the bedroom?"

D: "Yeah, I thought I felt the bed vibrating."

B: "He was there...Do you have ticklish feet?"

D: "Yes, he used to torture me by holding me down and tickling my feet."

B: "Did you write a verse for him?"

D: "Yes I wrote him a poem."

B: "Why does he keep taking me to a lake?"

D: "My parents live on a lake, and I am visiting them there this week."

B: "He liked it there, too. He liked getting away there in nature.

Did he not like grits or oatmeal?"

D: (I laugh) "Yeah! His mom just told me a story yesterday. She said he asked her to stop making oatmeal. She burned him out on it, how funny."

B: "He was there with you."

B: "Is it you or his mom with weakness in the eyes?"

D: "I am starting to have to adjust my focus with small type. I am afraid it's me."

B: "Who wants to swim with dolphins?"

D: "His mom. What is heaven like, or where he is at?"

B: "He is living by the river. He likes being with people, but he has built it a little bit away. He is growing orchids in the garden for you. He is nurturing a home for you together. He's got a white horse there. There must be significance of a white horse there. Darcy, I feel his energy pulling back. It was a great connection today. You are a lovely couple."

I was left speechless when a month after the dove appeared outside the house, a woman halfway across the world recounted the story. I was left with the permanent knowledge that Vern is part of something grand and can communicate very well to these special gifted people. Bernie hit on so much, and it was very specific information. The most important thing she told me was how deep our connection was. I felt that at the core of my being.

Journal Entry: Letter to Vern, June 18, 2009

Oh Mascorro,

Bernie brought me back to the moment eight years ago when we could have gotten together but something stopped us. The night you asked me to sleep over because you did not want to be alone. You were grieving over so many losses, your last relationship being one. I dream of the day that I can jump into the wormhole to go through time and change that decision. I remember the night vividly when I spent the night in your bed with you, comforting you. I wanted to be more than just your understanding buddy. I could feel that same need from you, but I could not act, I did not act. I was scared it was only my wishful thinking.

Why? So much would have changed if I was bold and said how I felt. I always feared rejection most of all from you. With you, the stakes were the highest. If I couldn't have you as my beloved, at least I had you as my best friend. I couldn't risk losing you.

Let me know if you find the path to the wormhole, if I could have another shot, I would most certainly take it.

I miss you my beloved,
Bellows

CHAPTER 16: SARA'S STORY— IF I CAN DO IT, ANYBODY CAN

I received an unexpected call from a family friend. I could hear the sadness in her voice. I hadn't spoken to her in several years; she lived in Minnesota, I in California.

"Hi Darcy, Carrie told me to reach out to you, she said that we have something in common." She then said that she had lost her boyfriend, and she felt so overwhelmed with sorrow.

"Oh my God, Sara! I am so sorry. This sorrow I know too well," I cried in empathy.

Sara then took me by surprise by saying, "I heard you are reading. Can you do one for me? I so badly need to hear from him."

I quickly responded, "No, I don't read, I am just trying to learn so I can communicate with Vern for myself. A message from your beloved is important. I wouldn't want to give you anything under the guise that I am connected, because I don't feel I am. And I don't take getting and giving messages lightly. I have had some phenomenal experiences but that's it. I will gladly gift you a reading with one of my newfound medium friends that I know is connected."

Sara replied, "Carrie said you have had lots of success reading in your circle."

I responded, "I've had fun and been surprised by some of the accuracy. I will get songs by people's favorite artists or a song that is particularly meaningful, and then I get random words that seem meaningful to the person but meaningless to me. That's it, Sara. It is important in your fragile state to get someone who knows with certainty that they are communicating with the other side."

Sara responded, "I hear you, but can you please just try?"

"Okay, but please don't judge what I get on whether a connection is possible. Remember, this does not necessarily make any sense to me. I have to meditate for a few minutes and will call you back with what I get."

During the following phone call:

D: "Okay, this is what I got, what I wrote on paper after meditation. Please remember I am not a medium, but I do believe we can all develop the skill.

Red, red tricycle."

S: "Oh my god. What did you say?"

D: "Red tricycle."

S: "Wow! Do you want me to tell you what it means?"

D: "No, not yet, let me finish...Runner."

S: "Okay."

D: "Swimming. Peppermint Patties."

S: "Really?"

D: "Yes. I feel slow dancing. Him looking into your eyes intently, his arms around your waist pulling you close. Jazz music. Marvin Gaye. I hear the song, 'What's Going On?' I hear a few of the lyrics you need to look them up.

I then hear Eddie Murphy singing "Lemonade that cool refreshing drink." I see a smile that lights up the room, very white teeth. I hear love at first sight. Could be an entertainer; center of attention.

He is sorry he could not reach out to you. His mind was not his own at the end. He is grateful for your time together. He understood the burden of his disease and does not want you to carry it. He is thankful you cared for him.

He knew you loved him, and he loved you. Learn from his tragedy. Understand how precious life is and live for today. Live for the moment.

He could be the entertainer, the center of attention—he is telling me he was a wise man.

Write all the unsaid things you wanted to say to him in a journal and then write what you think he would say so you will know.

He also wants you to stop smoking. (I thought this was just me because I could hear a smoker's voice.)

Playing with Preston…R name…Tall jagged mountains…I see overheating and sweat; you cool him off, refreshing him…7-Up…Pinball…I see a game and someone saying 'don't cheat'…Thai food…

And that's it. So now you can tell me how I did?"

S: "I can't believe you said 'red tricycle'. We met over a red tricycle. Preston and I were out in the driveway, and Preston was learning how to ride a tricycle for the first time. He couldn't get the pedaling part down. Kefa saw this from his driveway, so he walked over and crouched down and placed Preston's feet on the petals. Kefa spent the next couple of weeks teaching Preston how to ride."

D: "Wow, Sara, I can't believe it. There is no sensation to it for me, I just write down words, images, or feelings that pop in my head. I questioned Red Tricycle but I said it any way."

Sara proceeded to tell me their story. She had met Kefa that day, the day Preston was riding a red tricycle. The couple fell quickly in love in spite of the fact that Kefa was dying of a rare cancer. Sara said that Kefa was from Kenya, and he had a bigger than life smile and personality, somewhat like Eddie Murphy referenced in the readings. She said he had wisdom beyond his years. He was good with kids, and, while being treated for his disease, he still found the energy to play with and care for his nieces and nephews as well as her boy, Preston. This explained the game playing part of the reading.

Sara said that she and her mother became care providers for Kefa for a short time while he lived with them. And that her mother bought him peppermint patties to soothe his throat. She said the running was in reference to the people of Kenya always winning the marathons; it was an inside joke between them.

She said she knew he enjoyed music but would have to check on the jazz and Marvin Gaye reference with his sister-in-law. She said they had broken up a couple months prior to him dying, for which she felt a tremendous guilt. So she understood the personal message about the disease. She said that he often reminded her that she needed to stop smoking.

She called me the next day to tell me of interesting phenomena and to verify a few other points. She said that morning she awoke to an alarm of jazz music blasting that she had not set. This made her call Kefa's sister-in-law to ask some questions. Sara asked if Kefa liked jazz, and his sister-in-law said he did. Sara also asked about whether he liked Marvin Gaye, and was told that he did indeed like the singer.

More than the fact that he liked the song was the strength of the message in the music. I later found out that in 2007-2008, the year prior to Kefa's passing, Kenya went through a civil war. The Marvin Gaye song described civil war which is what the sixties were all about. I looked up the lyrics and was struck by the device spirit used to communicate the situation he was in. Kenya was in the civil war described by the song.

CHAPTER 17: HEAVEN AND HELL

I wonder what it is like for Vern in a bodiless form. Is he in heaven? I know he is not in hell. Though far from a saint, he was a wonderful, loving man. Is there even such a thing as a heaven or hell?

My belief is that heaven and hell are an invention of our own consciousness. If you die believing that you are going to hell, it will be waiting there for you. I think our journey continues when we cross. I do not believe in a punishing God or Father/Mother. I believe in a loving one. Vern also did not believe in a punishing God; his beliefs were similar to mine but with a Native American slant.

Dante Alighieri, a poet and philosopher from the 13th century, described heaven and hell in layers of ascension or descent. He said that sinners of like ilk hung together. When I read his Divine Comedy in high school, I pondered the possibility of heaven and hell and the hierarchy of sins. I remembered that Dante said the lowest level of hell was reserved for hypocrites. I always agreed with the vision that the hypocrites' hell should be the lowest. There is nothing worse than someone standing in judgment of others with a list of sins equally egregious.

In my studies, reading book after book, I found Dante's vision was not far from what those who have been given the gift of clairvoyance report today. I have heard that we are with like souls in soul groups (soul families). The soul groups are the people we see in our incarnation.

Excerpt from the book the Divine Comedy by Dante Alighieri:

Beatrice stares up at the noonday sun, and Dante does likewise for as long as he is able. When he drops his gaze it seems to him as if a second sun is illuminating everything. Dante finds that he and Beatrice have ascended to a sphere of celestial fire.

As Beatrice, Dante's Guide, brings Dante up to explore the realms of after-life, Dante describes the passage below as they enter the first realm of heaven.

They continue to ascend, and Dante feels himself to be pure light, pure spirit, and draws himself toward God with this feeling. Beatrice tells him that he is now rising up faster than lightning strikes down. She states that everything seeks its own level.

This is what we have all heard the death or near-death experience to be like. A light pulls you forward, a light with no fear. The theory is: you either choose to go in or you don't. I find it fascinating that a 13th century writer held the same vision. I felt it was necessary to get feedback from my most trusted soul in the universe, my beloved. I wasn't sure how I could validate that it was truly his feedback I was receiving, but I did my best.

I asked two trusted Mediums to answer questions, the same set or a similar set of questions, so I could compare the answers. I also asked Michelle on two different occasions a couple years apart.

D: "What did he see when he first crossed?"

M: "Dark then light. Darkness then light shadows of people."

D: "Did he recognize the people?"

M: "Some, they were all coming to greet him."

D: "Who was there?"

M: "Grandfather, great grandmother, grandmother. Is there a little boy? Because I'm seeing a little boy."

D: "Could be a few different people. Or others who were set to come but didn't."

M: "Vera, is there a Vera?"

D: "Yes, there is an Aunt Vera in spirit."

M: "I see people pat him on the back like they would after returning from war. I feel like this was wasn't right after the accident. I feel it was, like, after he came to terms."

D: "What does he do during the equivalent of a day?"

M: "He said he is doing whatever makes him happy."

D: "What makes him happy? "

M: "Visiting and helping others who are in the same boat."

D: "What is the 'same boat'?"

M: "In shock over their passing. I heard him say, 'I am Superman'. I am seeing him flying in to save the day."

D: "What is the other side as he knows it?
Is he in heaven?"

M: "It is a place that is of your free will, and it is your choice. It is your own reality. He said yes, he is in heaven."

D: "Has he met God?"

M: "We are all one. My writing is changing. It's big. Did he write big? We are all a part of God."

D: "Yes he often wrote big. Are there levels you are placed into by merit?"

M: "No."

D: "Is he with bad people?"

M: "Everyone is together."

D: "Does he have the same dangers there as we do here with bad people?"

M: "No."

D: "They can't hurt others?"

M: "No."

D: "How does he communicate?"

M: "There are no secrets. Everyone knows everything, they can merge together. The information is right there, riding like waves. He is showing me locking fingers together."

D: "Did he have a life review?"

M: "Yes."

D: "How was that?"

M: "It was his choice."

D: "Whether to see it or not?"

M: "It was very emotional and eye opening. It's not what he expected. He learned there was so much hurt caused by his actions."

D: "To himself or to others?"

M: "Others. Were there some bad relationships?"

D: "Yes."

M: "There was someone really hurt by something he did. Did he have a long-term relationship other than you?"

D: "Yes, that has to be Martine. It was his other significant relationship."

M: "A lot of fighting, a toxic relationship. One of those relationships where they love to hate each other. They had one good year as a couple and then it became something else."

D: "Yes, Vern told me exactly that."

M: "Vern didn't realize the damage done. Did he take it hard when Vern passed?"

D: "I'm not sure."

M: "He's blocking it out even though it's still there. That was a bad situation."

D: "Yes.

In books they talk about spirits leaving to go to a higher state of being."

M: "He said no levels."

D: "Do we reincarnate? "

M: "Yes, anyone can choose to come back at any time."

D: "Did he choose to come and abandon me?"

M: "No, no, no."

D: "When people choose to come back, do they also choose their role?

M: "We can choose the situation to come into to but not the outcome. We can choose a family."

D: "Is the outcome for us each to discover?"

M: "The outcome is not always a choice. With the accident he did not choose to go, he was forced into it."

D: "When a person comes back do they look the same?

M: "He said similar."

Jacqueline Q&A Channeling similar questions:

D: "Ask him to please provide specific and unique evidence to Darcy that this is Vern."

J: "One of his last holidays on earth, you were mad at him. He was in a bad mood and messed it up. He also shows an image of himself looking out a window. He says to think about that. Colorado may not prove that's Vern but I clearly hear Colorado. For no apparent reason, I am shown a red tootsie-pop. Just remember that I am told."

D: "What were the circumstances that lead to Vern's death?"

J: "Accident. I was shown an image of Vern looking down to get something and not looking at the road for a very short time. He could not believe it happened."

D: "Ask who Vern was to Darcy."

J: "Twin flame, true soul connection, I also hear 'husband'! He won't say you were engaged, he says husband."

D: "What did Vern see when he first crossed?"

J: "Colors, a range of colors, like a spectrum. I can also see people who greet him at some point but he goes to a 'healing room' whatever that is. I can hear voices at first and only see colors, feels like I am traveling through colors."

D: "Did he see or recognize any people? If so, who?"

J: "A male figure, a relative."

D: "What does he experience in the equivalent of a day?"

J: "A day does not exist there, there is no equivalent. But for the sake of the question, I am told he is in what appears to be a classroom of some sort and working on some projects. He seems very busy."

D: "Does he experience emotions and interactions with others? Does he have a job or things he would like to accomplish? If so, what?"

J: "He has several goals: coming up on communication levels to you, helping you complete your work so you can go home to him. Your goals are his goals. I also heard 'unity project' and I am shown a huge map pertaining to that, like blueprints. Lots of blueprints. He is involved in a few things now, wasn't always. He is taking classes, I see Serapis Bey teaching one and Sanat Kumara another. I hear the word 'kundalini', that's the connective energy to him. I am also told Mahatma Gandi is someone he consults with on the unity project."

D: "What is the other side as he knows it? Is he in heaven?"

J: "He is in a peaceful surrounding. He won't say heaven because you, his wife, are still on earth. He seems to be in a good place, but there was this adjustment I hear."

D: "Has Vern met God/Creator/Source?"

J: "He contacted energy, not a being."

D: "Are there levels that people are placed into by merit?"

J: "There is evolution and what a person has done for others. Overall, he did evolve on earth this time."

D: "Is he with bad and good people mixed together? Are both types with him?"

J: "He won't use good or bad with me, just says different people cross his path."

D: "Are there dangers, can anything hurt him?"

J: "No, not there. His emotions can still hurt, and he can still feel your emotions."

D: "How does he communicate?"

J: "Telepathically, sometimes does physical signs, wants to use imagery."

D: "Did he have a life review, and what was it like?"

J: "Very fast if using earth time but also overpowering. Emotional, good, but sad too. Felt what others felt for him. Felt the love you and others had, did not connect to all the love he had on earth."

D: "In books they talk about spirits leaving to go a higher state of being."

J: "Choices are made, the one harmonic? (He winks) That's about moving up in vibration. But he won't go to the one harmonic unless you join him. It's more complicated than books and they confuse vibration, frequency and the one harmonic."

D: "Do we reincarnate?"

J: "Yes."

D: "How does it work?"

J: "Individual, tailor made. It's a process of determining if and when a person should go. If that person has more to learn and hasn't overcome some things."

D: "Did he choose to go and abandon me?"

J: "No, I got a huge 'NO'!"

D: "Do we get a choice to come back and can we choose our role?"

J: "Yes, but it's more complicated than it appears."

D: "Are we predestined?"

J: "Some things are, but many are choices. It varies."

D: "When a person comes back do they look the same?"

J: "Some people do that, others don't at all. 'Individual' he says again with a smile. He is claiming he liked how he looked."

D: "Do we have free will in our earth life? Do we have it in the afterlife?"

J: "Yes, mostly. And yes."

The answers from the mediums were similar; though it was obvious each had their own filter. Many of the more complex questions had vague answers. I was comfortable with the experiences that were explained. I could be stuck on my own definition of heaven. My definition of heaven has me surrounded by loved ones; there is no pretense, no need for conflict because nobody is wanting it. We know we are loved, we know we are respected, we have no need to be validated by others.

CHAPTER 18:
DR. STANLEY'S TELEPHONE TO THE OTHER SIDE

I received an email from my friend Dr. Salo Stanley. She had some research to share with me. She was a true light worker in the world, and her work was to help others heal themselves by teaching them to create an environment of peace and well-being. She acted as a conduit for spirit. She charged modest fees, making her services accessible to anyone wanting to try something new to help heal them.

When I first met Salo, she was working on a phone booth to the other side. She had modified a radio called a Ghost Box or a Frank's box. It's a radio that scans stations at very fast rates. This radio reportedly allows spirits to communicate. Spirits manipulate the box by forming words with the sounds it scans or stopping on the words that were on the frequency. Salo had better results when using it then anyone I had witnessed before. She would bring the box along on investigations and it seemingly produced intelligent responses to questions. Yet, I still felt skeptical about the technology because sometimes it said random things when no question had been asked. It lacked the 'smoking gun' quality I needed to trust that it was real, though it definitely piqued my curiosity.

Salo had some different experiences to bring to the table. She believed in numerology, astrology, and the laws of attraction. She had a well developed sixth sense and was in touch with her spiritual guides. She certainly challenged my narrow belief system without challenging it directly. Salo had and innate knowledge of things most of us do not understand, and she trusted her instincts, or her guides as she called them.

In another life I would have thought she was crazy because she would share information and say my guides told me this or that. I started following what her guides where telling her, and, from a fact-based analysis, most of her (or their) predictions were very accurate. I started to believe that maybe guides are just as real as disembodied souls communicating through channels.

____

From: Salo Stanley Subject: mp3 Vern?
Date: Apr 17, 2011 3:10 PM

Darcy,

I did an EVP session in Feb of this year. My guides said this may be Vern's voice, is it? Around the 12 sec point, 'I'm Sorry' - the mp3 is attached.

Many Blessings,
Salo

____

Salo had a gift with science. She was part scientist and part alchemist. Even though I had originally thought the Frank Box was ridiculous when I saw it on TV, Salo seemed to have a magic touch with the radios she created. She got these boxes to clearly and regularly work. I had witnessed Salo receiving clear words and intelligent responses from her boxes during several investigations. I very excitedly pushed the play button on the mp3 she sent me.

S: "Any messages for Darcy from her sweetie?"

Box: (comes in fuzzy) "Fresno."

S: "Any messages For Darcy?"

Box: (comes in crystal clear) "I'm sorry."

S: "Are you?"

"What?" I said out loud. Oh my god, that is his voice! I couldn't believe my ears. I sprang up and looked around—there was no one I could share this with. I listened again and got shivers. I had received a reading in February, a few weeks earlier, where Vern apologized for all this happening. He said he was sorry, and I told him there was no reason to be sorry because he did not intentionally make this happen. He said he knew that, but he just felt so foolish. His attention was distracted for two seconds and it cost us our lives, our life together. I cried, I didn't want him carrying that load. He also felt the same sense of loss I felt. He did not want me carrying the load either. This recording was made in February. How did he do this, can he do it again?

I sent Salo an answering machine recording of Vern's voice to provide validation that it was his voice. When I first met Salo, she said it was one of her dreams to create a phone booth to the other side.

We repeatedly tried other sessions, and we got intelligent, directed answers. But we did not get his voice that clearly again, though it seemed like in the session he was trying to modulate the device. With each question, it seemed like he was adjusting the response lower to match his manly voice.

Why this message had his voice and later ones only answered questions intelligently, I don't know. Salo suggested that it takes a lot of energy and practice for spirit to manipulate the box, hence the inability to sustain the quality and length of connection. She said that Vern was learning just like we were.

I shared the connection with his mom and she was struck and instantly remembered a story from his childhood. She said that when Vern was pretty young, like nine or ten, they went to the movie ET together. There was a scene where ET, the alien, was trying to phone home through a conglomeration of radio and computer equipment. Vern was convinced that this technology could be made and researched it in his own way.

Journal Entry: Letter to Vern, April 18, 2009

Mascorro,

I got your message today via Salo's voice box session, and I am so very sorry too. The whys and the what-ifs are hard to overcome. I was told by a wise person in my widow group that it is not necessary to overcome it completely; you just cannot let it consume and rob you of future opportunities for joy. When I finally have you beside me, holding my hand from the spirit side, I will try. I know I can do it if you can do it.

Life is short in the scheme of eternity. If I know you will be there for me, I know I can do it for you.

Your voice, that voice that made me feel all girly inside anytime you spoke, oh the gift of hearing it one more time. I cannot explain what that means to me. I wish I could share it with you and see your beautiful face light up one more time. Who am I kidding? One more time will never be enough.

I love you eternally,
Bellows

CHAPTER 19:
IT'S THE PACKAGE THAT COUNTS

I awoke for the third night in a row from a bad dream. I kept dreaming that Vern was found alive and living in the town he used to live in before we got together as a couple. In the dream I was so elated he was alive and wanted to see him, but so utterly devastated that he obviously chose to leave me. I don't know why this was in my subconscious fears. It was not congruent with Vern's character, but the thoughts and images really bothered me. I tossed and turned, unable to get back to sleep. I took out my laptop and started my regular morning routine of reading my email.

I received a personal email from my new acquaintance, the author of the book I found after Michelle and I had met. Her name was Jacqueline Murray. She authored the book Tale of Two Brothers. She and I had become pen pals of sorts over the internet the past couple of years. She put me on her email list after I wrote her and told her how much I enjoyed her book. She knew my basic story that my beloved had died in car crash and that I was on a journey of discovery, hungry for information about the human spirit. So we shared information on spiritual topics.

Jacqueline wrote me and told she had a received a visit from Vern. He had asked her to send me something that was very important for me to receive. She asked for my address because she had no idea where I lived, just as I had no idea where she lived. I gladly obliged as I was very curious what Vern would ask her to send. I was still upset from the nightmare, so I paged through the movies on Netflix and I found What Dreams May Come. I remember a friend sharing it right after Vern passed, but I could not watch it because it was too much sadness to absorb. That night I played the movie, and it rocked my world.

It was about a family who had experienced horrific tragedy. First the kids die in a car crash, and then the father, and finally the mother by her own hand. From heaven, her husband watches his wife struggle with her inconsolable grief. In her last days on earth, he tries to communicate with her, "I'm still here..." at this point, I burst out in tears feeling the moment to be serendipitous. Vern was trying to tell me, "I'm still here". And what's more, the second half of the movie was about the husband leaving heaven to rescue his wife in hell. He was willing to stay there just to be near her. I knew this was the message my lover was sending to me.

———————

From: Jacqueline's email
Subject: Lots of information for you!
Date: Sep 6, 2011 3:27 PM

Hi Darcy,

Where do I start? Okay, here's what took place with Vern! I went through a lot with him over the weekend lol. Oh my goodness, but I think he is happy with what was sent.

The first thing sent is coming from a gift shop and he was very specific when I went through the designs on these things. It's a small item, and he did not tell me the meaning. So that one, you will need to ask him about it. It's on the way.

On Saturday night, he had me locate two things for you. Let me show you what they were as it will make sense to you now:

1) http://www.amazon.com/What-Dreams-May-Come/

I had it in my Amazon shopping bag. I was sending it to a new address, one I don't normally use on Amazon, which would be yours, and it required my credit card info to be entered in again. My purse was down in my car and I was tied up and could not get it at the time. When I did get my purse on Sunday night to send it, Vern came in and said, "No, no don't send it now." I thought WOW, I was sure he wanted that DVD sent to you, but I see why he didn't now, you watched it already!

The next item may be what the medium spoke of:

2) http://www.bradfordexchange.com/products/103424001_romantic-necklace.html

I thought this was so sweet and touching, he was very specific about a 'love letter' necklace. I started to search for one but on Saturday, in my mailbox, there was a Bradford Exchange catalog. Since I had not shopped with them previously that I can recall, it was very obvious to me I would find it there. And there it was. I thought it would be a beautiful thing to send you, but then Jim showed up with Vern!

On Sunday night, after being told not to send the DVD, I was still going to send the love letter necklace. Jim came in and sat down with Vern and I asked what was up and if everything was alright. Jim said, "Look Jacquie, Vern wanted to get Darcy something else other than the necklace but was afraid to ask you because of the money involved. But I told him, I thought you would do it." So out went the love letter necklace!

So I asked Vern what he wanted for you. He was very nice and said he didn't want to put me through any more trouble, and yes, it would cost me. But he would try not to wipe out my bank account lol. He told me what he wanted and so Vern and I went shopping yesterday!

I went to a store that was a big chain first, thinking they would have a nice variety of the item he wanted for you and he told me to turn around and go to an individually owned store. So I did, and I really worked hard to hear him and make sure I got what he wanted. He made a choice, a very, very nice choice. I had some questions about sizes and things and he told me not to worry about that, something can be done or it could be fixed. The item was one of a kind, they did not have another like it.

So we left the store and he tells me I cannot send it to you in that box, as it was in a plain box and I had to go home and find this particular box I was given a gift in last Christmas! I said, "I cleaned things out recently and I don't think I have the box anymore". And Vern said, "Yes, you do, Jacquie." He was right. It was on a shelf lol. So let me apologize up front for sending you a used box but he insisted it was sent in this box and not the plain box it came in. And it's not from Juicy Couture like the box says, and it's also not costume or fake, it's real! It had to be real for you. It's the shape of the box that mattered!

So to recap, two items are coming your way. One is from a gift shop and one is sent directly from me in Pittsburgh. Vern was quite anxious this morning for me to get the second item in the mail, and when I did, he asked me to request a signature on the package. So I did. You may get a note from the post office saying you may need to pick it up there and sign for it. Sorry about that, but it's one of a kind and it's very important to Vern!

Jacquie

____

Three days later, I received the package from Vern via Jacqueline. I opened it, and it was in a heart-shaped silk box. Vern loved packaging; he said it either increased or decreased the perceived value of any object. This package would meet his standards. I opened it to discover it was a wedding ring. I was in disbelief. I shook my head. Jacqueline did not know Vern and I were not yet married and even if she did, we were set to be married in three months. Most couples would have a wedding ring when they got engaged, but Vern was really belaboring the ring. He wanted it to be perfect, something so special no other couple would have it. That was my man, he was so grandiose. I told him something simple with a square cut diamond and white gold would be fine, but he was not convinced that was the way to go. This ring in the box was precisely to order.

From: Darcy Bellows
Subject: Words cannot express
Date: Sep 9, 2011 9:52 PM
To: Jacqueline email

My God, Jacquie, I am lost for words. I don't know what to say, but you are such a kind soul. I am crying because I am so deeply moved by your unbelievable generosity. I hardly feel worthy of such a kind act. Honestly, I could have won a new multi-million dollar mansion and it would have meant less to me than this.

The story behind the ring is that Vern did not get a chance to buy me an engagement or wedding ring before he died (we were to be married in three months). We were economically repairing everything and he wanted to find just the right piece. He was very romantic and wanted to find something special, something to express what he termed our sacred love. No average ring would do for my beloved. For me, I had the biggest prize: his love and honor, no girl could ask for more. He couldn't find the befitting piece before he was taken from this plane of existence.

Vern was a merchant and active in the city council and local business revitalization efforts. He owned his own business and would never buy something significant from a chain. Your story, down to the detail of him insisting on getting a signature with the post office, was so much his personality—his store was named Postal Xtra. I remember sending out Christmas packages, and he insisted on getting the signature because he knew how the Post Office could lose things.

I also have to tell you that Sunday night I received a gift from my friend Salo in Fresno. She gave me the voice box that she captured Vern's voice on EVP and told me to try for myself and taught me how to use it. Then I came home to get your email with the request from Vern and Jim.

I am humbled by your altruistic heart. I aspire to be...Jacquie you are truly a rare breed, an earth angel.

I hope we can meet one day in person.

Sending Love, may you be blessed with the gifts you have given and so much more!

Darcy and Vern (from the other side)

——————

How could Vern search the world to find someone unselfish enough to donate a wedding ring from a spirit to his beloved left here? What are the odds? Do we all of a sudden become all knowing, or can we tap into the source of all knowing? Why would one ever leave that state if they didn't have to?

CHAPTER 20:
THE FOREST THROUGH THE TREES

A holiday or birthday is never the same; one of the chairs is always empty at our table. I now get to live with the knowledge that Vern was with us, that he sees everything. This made my suffering a little less. Vern had given me so much proof that I knew he was always there looking after me, his mom, and the girls. I get to live with the knowledge that our soul, our essence, is infinite and that we never really lose our connection to the people we love so dearly.

Each holiday, each birthday, I had to see the despondent look in the back of Henri's beautiful eyes. She wanted to believe that all the signs she received were real: the dove, the swinging dream catcher, the countless messages I sent through to her. Many of Vern's friend's also had dreams. She had what I know were intuitive messages. We both wondered why we did not have dreams.

I told Henri that when she was ready, she would have a reading. On the second birthday after Vern passed, Henri was finally ready. Vern and I, before his passing, were already talking about what to do with this milestone birthday. It was his mom's big 60th birthday. Now, somehow, it didn't seem appropriate to celebrate in the style her son would have wanted because it would be a painful reminder of the magic that celebration was missing.

I could not think of more appropriate way to celebrate her 60th birthday than to connect Henri to her son. She needed to know this was not the end of their sacred relationship. When I finally got the word she was ready, I did not hesitate to call Vickie Gay and arrange the reading for her birthday.

I just knew Vern would come through and give her exactly what she needed to hear most. I always shared bits of what I received in my readings and it was exactly what I needed to help me through, to get me to believe, to get me to the next step. I said to her, "Vern always knew what to say in life. I trust he will know what to say to you from beyond. When I received my first reading, I needed to believe it was him with highly personal specific facts that no stranger could possibly know. Then I needed to hear what happened from his perspective, and I needed to understand how he felt. I also needed to know he would not leave my side." All of this was delivered and more. I couldn't wait to hear what Vern would have in store for his most beloved mother.

I knew Vickie—who had relatives that were from Henri and Vern's tribe—would be the right reader for Henri's first reading. Henri's reading started out with specific evidence, a snippet or scene from Vern and Henri's life together. A piece of red cloth, which she said was long and that she saw unfold. We both were looking at each other questioning it like we did not know what she was talking about. Vickie repeated the bright red cloth part and said it was carefully, almost reverently, being folded. She said he is not making it go away so you need to acknowledge it properly. We shrugged and said maybe it will come up later, and then the next piece tied it together for us. Vickie described a sacred native ceremony with the drum beat and then Henri got it. She said it was her Native American shawl that she used to dance with at sacred rituals, and said Vern helped her pick the fabric. It was the same shawl she danced with at his crossover ceremony, the same shawl he was overwhelmed with pride and joy seeing his mother dance with.

She then described a big water basin that sits outdoors, "It's shaped like a big cement bowl, you see them outside." I suggested a water tower. She replied, "No, something like a hot tub. It's a place."

We looked at each other like 'I don't know'. She described it again as round and filled with hot water. I said they have a hot tub that they haven't used in years. Vickie said that wasn't right. She told us not to forget it, it's important. Vickie was trying to describe what she was seeing, but she had not actually visited this place before so she did not know what it was. Lo and behold Mike was setting up a slideshow to show me of the vacation they had just taken in Mammoth. After the reading, we stepped aside to watch it. The very first few pictures were of hot springs with a bowl like hot tub placed in to collect the hot sping water which fit the description completely. Vickie had relayed it perfectly!

I said to Henri, "Oh my God that is the big hot water basin Vickie was describing. Vern was trying to tell you he was there."

"You're right Darcy," she replied. She shook her head.

Henri's reading got much more personal from there, she was snapped into an absolute knowing when Vickie repeated a conversation that Henri had with her son. Vickie relayed a conversation from the day Vern asked his mom how he would know if he found the one he was destined to be with, if there was such a thing. He was considering our marriage and he wanted to make sure I was 'the one'. He said, "You said that she should be someone I can trust, someone who will always stand up for me no matter what, someone who will protect my heart like her own. Someone who is truthful and someone who I truly enjoy being with. I found all of that in Darcy. I know it's strange to be talking about her now in front of her but I need you to know she is the one and she can be trusted."

Vickie continued to deliver the message to Henri in the first person as the tears streamed down our faces. "Mom you have to stop thinking of things that did not happen, all those negative thoughts, thoughts of things that did not happen." He said, "You need to follow your own wisdom and your own advice and not focus on negative thoughts. What you are thinking might have happened did not happen. I was just as shocked as you."

This was a conversation between Vern and his mom. I was not sure exactly what was being talked about, but Henri knew exactly what he was saying. She cried, nodded, and said yes. All of this was Vern's words straight from Vern's consciousness to his mom. He was aware of his mom's private thoughts and fears.

He spoke directly to them through the Medium. He comforted her by speaking to her worst fears, the fears that plagued her mind. These questions would have remained unanswered if not for this gift. This was her son, the boy and then the man who always spoke directly to his mom. He knew she needed peace of mind, so he spoke to what troubled her the most and the 'what-ifs' she was obsessing over. A bit of relief accompanied Henri's sorrow. She knew it was really her son. Her words said it all: "My son, you continue to teach me but I cannot teach you anymore". As Henri said this I cried, and she cried.

I cried tears of joy and sorrow for I could never really give her what she wanted which would be to have her son here with us and to be able to teach him. She wanted her son to live and die in natural order. She wanted to be the one to deliver her son the message from heaven after a rich full earthly life. At least she now knew that Vern really was beside her.

Journal Entry: Letter to Vern, October 29, 2011

Mascorro,

Oh my love, you sent such a beautiful message to your mom. She has been waiting a while to hear exactly what you told her. We are both so lucky for your love. I want you to know what I have learned from you.

We are more than the sum total of our things and others' perceptions of what we are. Only love without fear and reservation can bring true happiness. You taught me the value in being an optimist. You taught me that my view of things wasn't the only way, that if I opened my mind and heart to new things and other ways of thinking, I would surely grow. You taught me that even bad experiences can make you a better person.

I remember all of the different ways you took me out my comfort zone and helped me grow into a better person. I want to say to everyone I meet, 'Cherish the differences, observe and grow'. Growth, that's what we are here for. The only death we have is that of stagnation. Even in a time when I want to lay down, you are in another dimension challenging my assumptions, ensuring I move forward. You did this for your mom too.

I love you so much Mascorro!
Bellows

One early morning in a life that seemed so far away now, my wonderful life before Vern died, I awoke to Vern's gentle touch on my face. He said, "I want to take you for a drive. I want to get out of the city and clear my head in nature. Let's just get out of here and drive to wherever the road takes us." I agreed, still half asleep. I knew adventures with Vern meant a mind-blowing good time or a life-altering learning experience.

"Should I pack anything?"

He said, "Nope, we need nothing but an open mind and an open heart." He winked.

We took my little baby blue VW convertible bug. He said to drive it you had to be comfortable with your masculinity because it was a definite 'chick car'. We took the top down and headed east on the 580. I said anxiously, "Where are we going?"

He said, "Wherever the Highers lead us."

We stopped and got our favorite Starbucks, then hit the road. We started talking, and I lost track of time. We had driven for an hour when I leaned over and whispered, "You make me so happy." He snapped a picture. I hated getting my picture taken, so I bit his ear. To my surprise, he liked it and took four more pictures.

Vern then spoke a little more seriously, "We have known each other for 25 years. You know more about me than anyone else on earth. I haven't shared my spiritual side with you only because I never knew how to process it. But us natives are very connected to the earth, and some more than others."

He pointed to a large eagle soaring above on the tree line. "We have been following that eagle for the last 25 miles. It is starting to lower, so that is where we are going."

"Where is that?" I asked, chuckling snidely. "I think he is quite a ways ahead of us."

Vern ignored my tone and said, "I don't know, but I will know when we arrive." Vern drove for what seemed to be 10 more miles.

I was baffled. We couldn't see the eagle anymore. It had lowered. "Are you bull-shitting me? We haven't seen the eagle in a while, where are we going for real—you have a destination in mind don't you?"

This time he replied agitated, "Bellows, sometimes you can be such an asshole. I am telling you a truth I have not shared with you—part of my being because I was afraid of judgment, and now you deliver it on cue." I looked at him and could tell he was not joking and I suddenly felt like the asshole he just called me.

"I am sorry, babe. I thought you were joking. It's clear you are sharing something deep that I need to pay attention to. I didn't mean to make light."

He could tell I genuinely felt bad, so he pulled my hair to make light. We exited, took a left, and then he said no, it should be a right so he flipped a U. We took a left and then another left and we arrived at a park with a bunch of tents. He said, "This has been a Pow-Wow since I moved up here. I have not done much in the way of connecting. What you just witnessed is my ancestors calling me home. Do you know what a Pow-Wow is?"

"No love, you have never taken me to one before this."

He explained, "It's the native Indian way of prayer and celebration, a gathering of tribes to show reverence for what is. The fact that we were led here is in response to a need for me, and I am glad to share it with you as two become one."

This was one of many spiritual experiences Vern shared with me. It was like I had my own private shaman. I wondered where he got all this wisdom. He was the same guy who got me so drunk in a club one night that he had to carry me out and clean me up. Upon awakening the next morning in the bathtub, I was so humiliated. He told me then that I would be the talk of the town for the next day or so. I asked what I had done and said I was so sorry. He said, "You had fun. No one should judge you for that. If that bothers the town, fuck 'em!

CHAPTER 21: THE HINDU SAGE

Ordinary life is hard to get back into once you realize there is so much more to our being than collecting and co-collecting stuff. I tried to separate my work which for the moment was just a way to pay for my stuff. I did have enriching work experiences in the past, but it was almost like the deck was cleared so I would have time to pursue and cultivate my spiritual world.

I tried to find ways to incorporate spiritual growth and connection into my days, which proved to be very challenging. My energy was often drained after a day of people being upset by things we should not let pull us down. I got just as caught up, but for me it was doubly draining since I knew better.

After getting home from a particularly taxing day of meaningless tasks, I stared at the blank screen a while to dump the contents of my day—no luck, no peace in the electric glow. I took a deep breath and walked outside to the deck, the deck that opened up to another world. This world that God/Source/Nature had created. My apartment set atop of a mountainside, the deck had a view of green mountains playing peekaboo and a view of the ocean. The fog was rolling in over the top of the mountains. It took over the blue sky at a rapid rate.

There was a family of great big vultures that often visited, and two of them started circling and getting very close to the deck. I wondered what secrets they held as they swooped down from the heavens. I remembered that Vern could communicate with the eagles. "Will you send a message to my baby in heaven?" I thought to myself, "I love you, let me know you can hear me."

I left my trouble behind at the thought of riding the vultures to heaven to see Vern. I turned the laptop back on and picked up my mail. I received a message from a woman who said she used to work for Vern and she had just found out about his passing. She wondered if I would call her because she had a story to share. I loved sharing stories about my love; he was such a character. Anyone who knew him had a really good tale to tell about Vern. When you were with him, the worries of reality suspended and the magic began.

The woman's name was Lorena and she seemed as excited to talk to me as I was to her. She thanked me for calling. I thanked her for reaching out. She said, "I found you after I had a dream of Vern. He told me he died in the dream, so I looked up his name and found you. He was talking straight to me. He said he had died in an accident and to get in contact with his mom. I said, 'I can't remember your mom's name'. He then said 'Henri, stupid'. I laughed because I could hear him saying it." She laughed and said he could be so rude, funny and direct. She also said that though he was a tough boss, there was plenty of kindness and self-empowerment that he taught her. I knew instantly this was someone that knew him.

She also told me that she had always had the gift of seeing spirits, and when she found out I was writing a book about Vern, she felt some acceptance that she had never felt. She felt maybe the gift wasn't evil after all. She explained that her family made her feel that this gift of seeing the dead was not a good one and must be extinguished. I told her in my experience that could not be true because it was an incredible healing gift of love. It had to be from a benevolent source. I told her, "Though I grieve his physical presence, I feel so much peace because I now know we are connected. And I know he will be there for me always. I have also received the gift of another conversation. I got to hear things I needed to hear to help me through this most difficult of experiences."

Lorena then said, "Darcy, I have to tell you about a man who came to visit us in the office when I was working for Vern. We were still in the first smaller location. We were talking about getting the bigger office across the street when this Indian man in a white robe walked in.

He said, 'Excuse me, sir, but I need to talk to you,' to Vern. 'I am a seer and I need to tell you what I see for you.'

Vern said, 'Oh, no thank you. I don't believe in that stuff.' Vern wasn't buying what he was selling.

The man responded in a more urgent tone. I really need to speak to you about your future.

Vern replied, 'OK, go ahead.'

'We should do it in private,' the man said.

'Not necessary,' said Vern.

So the man went on to say, 'Young man, you are now in your glory days, an important man around town. If you stay on your path, you will lose everything and fall into despair. You will fall into the deception and dependency of drugs. After that I see you will die in fatal car accident before you are 40.'

Vern replied, 'Lucky for me, I don't believe in any of that.' Vern thanked the man for his concern and shook his hand and walked him out."

Lorena said that they had a good laugh at the man's 'prophecy' because Vern was the least likely man to fall into drugs, in most people's opinions. He felt drugs were for the weak. Lorena said she had heard rumblings that this had happened a few years back but she found it very difficult to believe.

I was stunned. Chills went up and down my spine. A couple years prior to Vern and I finally getting together as a couple, he had spent almost five years in exile from all the people he held dear in his life. He had gone through a break-up, lost his business, fallen into debt, and then into drugs. This was an outcome nobody expected in Vern's life, least of all Vern. At the time of this man's prophecy, Vern thought him absurd, and he walked the man off the property. I vaguely remember Vern mentioning this event but he seemed more irritated than concerned and never mentioned the full details.

When I called Vern's mom, Mike remembered the event. He did not remember the details of the prophecy, but did remember the man coming in and leaving quite an impression on Vern. I also remember the summer before his accident he had a fear of dying in a car crash. This led me to more confusion than ever.

Journal Entry: Letter to Vern, November 9, 2011

Mascorro my love,

I am so confused about the seer who had 'warned' you of your tragic fate. Maybe the truth is that we are not meant to know. We are here to experience and grow. I know you would have something wise to say or a wise crack, one of the two. And either way the point is the same.

I must rededicate myself to hearing you for myself. I need more answers, and I need them from you. I know it's possible but not easy. My world gets consumed by distractions that keep me from hearing you.

I saw a couple in their 80s going to dinner at one of my favorite restaurants. The size difference with this couple was much like ours. The man stood almost a foot taller than his lady. I watched them interact for a moment. Though he was slow, he still had the will and the strength to gallantly take care of his wife. He opened her door, took her hand, and supported her back with his other arm to assist her out of the car. They held hands as they walked forward. The dumb smile on my face must have tipped the couple off that I was being reminded of something, though they did not know it was a reminder of what would not be. They both said hello and asked if I was coming from the restaurant. I replied, "Yes, it is one of my favorites." The gentlemen replied, "Yes, I am sure you and your husband will enjoy many favorite spots, just like me and Tess." I nodded to the sky and said, "I suppose you're right, have a lovely night."

I sometimes wonder who has it worse, you or me. You live with the knowledge of your loved ones' struggle without you. I get occasional glimpses of your feelings through the eyes of another who is more spiritually connected than I am, with their filter applied, of course.

Mascorro, you are the most amazing man I have ever known, I will love you eternally. I look forward to the day I can see you again. Until then, I'll be dreaming my dreams with you. And no, I have no intentions of getting over you, but I do plan to expand my view of reality and what is possible. I just ask that you hold my hand even it's only my etheric hand.

Yours Eternally,
Darcy Bellows (Mascorro)

CHAPTER 22: UNTIL WE MEET AGAIN

A couple of days after I learned of the mysterious sage who seemed to predict Vern's death, I was struggling with the concept that there was somehow a fate that could be seen and could have been prevented.

I couldn't stop thinking about the what ifs and whys. Vern was a human. Why would he have to walk the super human path in order to avoid a gruesome early demise?

I screamed in the car on the way home from work, "Mascorro, is there a God, is there justice? Baby, why? Could we have saved your life by walking a different path? I cried, and the tears streamed down. I felt despair again almost as if the wound was new.

As I walked into the apartment building, there was an orange, yellow, and black native bracelet put together with string hanging around the door knob to the apartment building. The color and pattern were an exact match to a few of the beaded pieces Vern owned. The bracelet contained the color of the Morongo tribe that Vern's uncle belonged too. I picked it up and pulled it toward my chest and looked up to the sky. "Mascorro, did you send me this?" I felt a warm feeling of comfort like he was trying to comfort me and my tears. The skeptic inside me only allowed a minute of relief. In spite of everything I had seen, old habits die hard. My mind switched, and I thought to myself, "Oh, someone probably dropped it." I placed it back on the doorknob, everyone in the building had to go through this door to get to their apartment. I declared to my beloved, "If this was meant for me it will still be here in a couple days."

I came home each night for three days, and every night it was still hanging on the knob. On the third night I pulled it off the knob. Once again, like a crazy person, I talked to the air, to my beloved, and accepted his gift by thanking him and bringing it inside with me. Feeling sentimental, I put it on the pillow beside me. It was too precious to wear. What if it fell off? I accepted it as just another mystery in this life that I will probably never understand.

Journal Entry: Letter to Vern, November 11, 2011

Mascorro,

First thank you for the gift. Darling I need a clear answer please send me one. Why did all of this happen to us? Were you predestined to leave me to die young?

I have so many unanswered questions. Were you fated to leave me? I cannot bare that thought! My love I don't understand. I feel like I was becoming a better person because of you and our union. I know that you told me you felt that same way, why then were you taken in the best part of our lives? Is there no justice? Is earth life hell and when we evolve we transcend? Is that why I am stuck here without you! I am sorry baby I do not understand this. Can you help me to understand. I know if we were talking in person you would explain everything to me. Do you have any answers? I wish I could hear your reply.

I miss you baby,
Darcy

____

I asked my now good friend Jacqueline to channel a response to this letter that I wrote and symbolically sent to Vern's email account but did not share with her.

Jacqueline's response and channeled letter from Vern seemed almost catered to my questions:

This is not the letter I wanted to do for you, sister. In fact, it totally freaked me out because, to me, this was not at all what you wanted! But Vern came through to me while I was asleep, and actually grabbed my shoulders and asked me to PLEASE give you what I was given! I also saw a black and white cat around him which made no sense. I recall you telling me he was a dog person. He was sitting at a table with a ceramic coffee mug, and I am not sure what was in it. I asked about the cat, and he told me you caused him to appreciate cats.

Okay hold onto to your seat, it's unbelievable:

Channeled Letter from Vern

Darcy my wife,

This is not the letter you asked for, but it's certainly what you want to know. Why? I am going to tell you, sweetie, but please keep in mind, this is not for the book, it's for you. Let me start by saying this, if you think I loved you a great deal on earth, beyond words, it's so much more now. It's immeasurable. I live for you, my soul continues for you, and that should pretty much cover it.

Why did I leave first? Was it a freak accident? I think you better really get ready for this. I know it seemed like a freak accident, babe, but I was answering your call. I know you will say you never would have wanted me to leave, we had so much to do and so much life to live. But you have to hear me out, and you have to be patient in getting this all down, it's not going to be easy.

We are a team babe, you and me, forever and always. We actually agreed to, or took this assignment, that we in fact created ourselves. To come to earth and pull back the veil, creating something we knew many lifetimes ago: there is no wall between those occupying human bodies and souls without them. We knew this because we lived it before, and we came with this assignment.

But we were busy living our lives, and I came close to death before. And yet, since we all have five exit points, I was not at my fifth and believe it or not, it wasn't written in stone that I would go first. One of us was going to leave much earlier than the other and create this journey for both. You had your girls, and they still need you, for now. You were also—and I hate to admit this—in some ways the more stable one, let's say, or the less bi-polar one. I was the restless soul. If you had left me first, it's common knowledge that I would have spiraled downward, nosedived, met the wrong woman who I didn't love, and wrecked her life too. I was not strong enough to go on without you on earth, and you must forgive me for that, Darcy.

I am seated on a swing seat now, and I am waiting for you to join me. I mean join me, where you can see me, hear me, and feel me put my arm around you or kiss you. You and everyone else wanting to visit their loved ones who are out of their human bodies can actually do this by going up in vibration, and it's not nearly as hard as the world would have you believe.

I am not talking about visitation dreams but a semi-trance or meditative state. You are here to learn how to do it and come spend time with me. Then teach others how to continue their relationships with their loved ones in this dimension. You can teach tens of thousands, if not millions. Jacqueline does this now, Darcy. She doesn't know how, but you can do it, and so can everyone else for the most part.

There are those who will say 'when you are dead, you're dead' or 'life is for the living', but the soul is more alive than any other part of a being, so this needs to be brought to light too. Stop them from the ignorance, that's what you are asked to do.

It was decided on a soul level that I was going to leave first. It was not clear as to when, as there is a time frame that extends a bit. The accident was more or less created to provide me an exit, a quick one, and one that would cause you to start the journey extremely rapidly. I was trying to get my phone that had fallen on ground because I was receiving a call from you. It's not a coincidence, it's because I was answering what you and I needed to do. Please stay with this, there is more to unfold here.

I left, and then you began your new journey. Here is the thing you haven't found yet but you must find for us. Darcy, you can do this. You are on earth now to pull the veil back and create a way that anyone, including you and me, can be together when someone leaves their human body. Most mediums will say this cannot be done because they want to believe they are special. But, in truth, it can be done. You will do it and have me back in your daily life in communication, and we will complete our journey on earth so you can finally get home, girl! You are not just there to teach about life after death or how you search for answers or receive them. You are there to show people that without being a yogi, or a guru, they can pull the veil back, safely, and in a way that all can do it. You had to go on this journey for years, in grief and pain, to see how desperate one becomes to receive communication. You had to feel this, baby, but we can fix this.

Can you imagine what you will be able to do to the grieving process? Can you even begin to realize, babe, how life-altering this will be to all the people missing their loved ones? It's not imagination, either, because the loved ones can give them things that are going to happen in the future, or things they don't currently know about. This will prove it's not imagination.

Now how are we going to do this? You are going to have to study about something called EMDR, and I mean study it. Then you are going to have work on vibration, and the key will be in the golden ratio to raising it. You will want to do Carol Tuttle's energy work on the chakras, and you will receive the keys to unlock the door. Once it's unlocked, you are asked to hand the keys to everyone. That's the purpose to me leaving first. It wasn't ideal, and it wasn't easy for anyone. Though I did not feel physical pain, it took me awhile to understand this and accept this and move forward. It wasn't instantaneous. My soul was always so restless, it wanted to blast off and somehow I knew it would. My greatest happiness was in that last year of my life with you. But I am not far away, in another world, on another side. I am in a different dimension, but there is basically no wall that comes between us.

No one on earth is really teaching this, but we have to. That's the reason I am in this dimension which is on top of yours, or three feet apart, and you are still there. You aren't there to work your mundane job or talk to mediums, you are there to find me, to connect back to me and teach others how to. Mediums will not be necessary anymore, Darcy. Third party communication has been important to us, I know this, but it's not ideal. Our relationship is intimate and I want it back! I don't want this thing where you talk to me and cannot hear me. It's not impossible, it's not far-fetched, it's achievable with time and discipline and yes, you will need to find the time so we can do this in weeks, not months.

There are also things I can answer and things I can't. Why? Darcy, everything is not meant to be known until one exits the human body. That's why very little is known. I mean it's a small amount compared to what happens. You judge yourself in your life review, you feel everything you made others feel, but there is so much more to it than that. You literally go and remove parts of your soul DNA that no longer serve you, lots of negative stuff. This is permanently deleted. You cannot bring it up or recall it once you have learned the lesson. We do not keep everything and carry it and exist with it. We remove what no longer serves us. An interesting dilemma for a medium when he or she asks for specific information, perhaps it's gone forever. I have not deleted one ounce of our life, Darcy. I have it all, even my bad moods, my depression, and other things. But when you come to this dimension, I will need to let some of that go. Excess baggage weighs down the plane.

There is so much going on in this dimension. But it's not for all on earth to know because it's too much information and very few people can even comprehend what this is all about. People will want to create a way to directly ask their loved ones. Mediums seem to like to go to the death, and that's good verification I guess, but enough about my crossing. It's a sore spot with me because I didn't live it. I was already in this dimension, so it's like watching a movie.

I wasn't to have another love after you, and I want you to be happy no matter what. But only someone who will see your beautiful soul and treasure you and the family will be allowed in the door. I would've ruined some woman's life if you left first. I wouldn't have loved her and she would have tried to help me so much she would've lost herself. We can still have dates. You just have to learn how. And yes, it can go into astral travel, and we are not talking about being asleep either.

I know it seems like a large task, but it's our destiny. And yes, it will change the world. You know I didn't come to earth not to end up changing the world. Yes there are many questions with this, how does someone move on if they are always communicating with their crossed over loved one? Let me see, they are living. They just don't see a wall. There is no divide and the love never stops. What is moving on? Having a new man or woman in your bed? Or going to the next level of personal and soul evolution? I realize the controversy but this is the time, and it's the time for us. Life didn't stop for either of us even if we wanted it to. Do you want me back with you in a way that you can communicate with me, see me, feel me and enjoy me to the fullest? Or should we keep going through this agony? You realize it's such agony for souls in this dimension, they often give up trying to send signs or communicate? You are going to set the humans free as well as the souls who have crossed as only you can. The humans, unfortunately, have to come up in vibration and learn how to connect. We are the lock, you guys have the keys. Will this change the entire book? I hope so. The final chapters about this process you will achieve have not yet been experienced and written. The journey as a whole should be told, though.

I have been waiting to explain this to you. No medium would even understand it or maybe even buy it. I have been waiting to tell you what this was all for and what needs to be done. I have been longing to get this out. It had to be done in time. I know you will say it didn't have to be the way it was, and that's true. But knowing us as I do, we chart great things. Do you think it was all a coincidence you were guided to a book and then to Vickie right after I crossed? I don't think so. You think it was just something in the air that made you connect to Jacqueline here, think about it. There was an outline created to this journey. It could have gone a thousand different ways, but for us to complete what we came to do, I had to leave early. There was a point to my early exit and gruesome death. There is a huge point to this journey, and you have to go way beyond finding some medium or discovering life after death. Which by the way, I denounce life after death anyway. Death of a human body is not really death, it's a shedding of skin.

I was not my skin. I was and am ever your mate, your one and only in truth, and you are mine forever. We have gone before each other in other lifetimes, and it was never easy. But we have met our goals and brought truth and light to the universe before, and we have to do it this time. Religion brought in fear and control and depression. We need to remove this fear and this concept of the division of dimensions. We need to teach people they can sit next to Jesus one day while still in a human body and learn from him or from Buddha or whomever. They can, and they don't have to be born 'psychic'.

I am now always around someone known on earth as Black Hawk, as we are currently walking our path together. This is not the letter you wanted, but it's the truth. And it's time to reveal the bigger picture and accomplish it so you can be back where you belong, where I am.

Yours Eternally,
Vern

____

This channeled letter was a lot for me to believe and absorb. Was I crazy in my spiritual state? Who am I?

I am just a girl who was enjoying physical life and all its lessons with an extraordinary man. I am angry with my spiritual self if I agreed to leave the incredible life I was finally having with Vern for one of subtlety and mystery. I do not have the ability to teach about the veil. What is a veil? I need more training, more success. I have no influence on anyone. I am not sure anyone does or should. I only know a small group of people.

This does not seem the least bit plausible. I can share my story to help gather other seekers and help look for bigger answers for ourselves. We can share stories and heal our grief together and be open to any enlightening experience, which is always better shared and witnessed. I fell asleep with many thoughts. I was puzzled by the letter. Was I reading it wrong? I know the reader. She delivered me a wedding ring from Vern; she is truly a selfless woman. All the thoughts were too much. I was exhausted by my own train of thought and finally fell asleep.

I awoke deeply disturbed by the dream I just had. I dreamt of a boy walking outside on an ice covered lake in wintertime. His father was on the shoreline yelling at him to come back at once, he had gone too far. The boy made an immediate about-face and headed toward his concerned father. He started to pick up speed and run when the ice broke apart underneath his feet. He fell into the freezing water, and then the ice shifted again covering the hole he had just fallen through. His father screamed helplessly on shore and dropped to his knees.

I then shifted my consciousness and felt like I was the dying boy. He crossed instantly and painlessly. As he left his body, he felt nothing but protection and warmth. As he ascended to his new state, this process felt like he was floating on a cloud. Sheer comfort and security, a bit like drifting into sleep snuggled in a comfortable blanket. There were other spirits there waiting to receive him. I saw Vern there with a fur-lined coat to wrap the boy in. Vern knelt down to his level and gave him a hug. As I started to awaken I wanted to return so I could find the father and tell him what I saw. As I gained full consciousness I said out loud, "I wonder who will help the dad?" I continued, angry and upset by the thought. Who is there to help the father survive what he had witnessed? Who was there to give him a blanket?

I am now upset by the thought of the inconsolable man, the father in my dream. I choose to divert my attention, my sad thoughts of this man, by turning on the TV. The program that illuminates the screen is a talk show honoring everyday heroes. A man helped save another man's son. A connection formed that was as great as any romantic love story.

At this point the magic, the message, does not elude me.

Vern is on the other side helping another man's son.

I need to help the father the survivor.

I need to show him how to find his son.

Like I found Vern, myself, and greater meaning.

Made in the USA
San Bernardino, CA
25 January 2014